C000100011

LIFTING OFF

By Karen McLeod

In Search of the Missing Eyelash

LIFTING OFF

Karen McLeod

MUSWELL
PRESS

First published by Muswell Press in 2024
Copyright © Karen McLeod 2024

Typeset in Bembo by M Rules

Printed by CPI Group (UK) Ltd, Croydon CR0 4YY.

A CIP catalogue record for this book is
available from the British Library

ISBN: 9781739193072
eISBN: 9781739193089

Karen McLeod has asserted her right to be identified
as the author of this work in accordance with the
Copyright, Designs and Patents Act 1988.

Apart from any use permitted under UK copyright law,
this publication may not be reproduced, stored or transmitted,
in any form, or by any means without prior permission
in writing from the publisher.

Muswell Press
London N6 5HQ
www.muswell-press.co.uk

For my sister Dawn,
and my love, Minnie

'We are what we pretend to be, so we must be careful about what we pretend to be.'

— **Kurt Vonnegut**

Prologue

With the unsettling dark ocean below, I could've been anywhere, my body set to any clock. The only constant was the drumming hangover in my head. I had to disguise this to the passengers and the act of doing so, of presenting normality, felt familiar and safe. Soon the alcohol would wear off, somewhere between the meal service and the duty free, and the trick was not to speak loudly in case they caught the whiff on my breath.

It had become a uniform in itself, this unintended life, and it was now well-tailored and seamless. We were halfway to New York, the plane a Boeing 767 which didn't exactly rattle, but belonged to the era of Cinzano ads and a meal trolley with a roasted joint of ham served by a stewardess. We were called cabin crew these days, and I was handing out drinks in the aisle, all eyes on what I might have in my drawers (I had to pretend to enjoy innuendo) when the captain announced over the Tannoy, *Will the Senior Cabin Crew member report to the flight desk immediately?*

'Red wine? Of course sir.' I handed over two miniature bottles, clicked the brake, lowered my eyes as I retreated from the cabin. It was exhilarating to break the routine, to be allowed to leave rows of passengers high and dry without a drink or a paper menu.

The purser appeared, then told us to prepare for an emergency briefing. We gathered round and she reported the captain had informed her there was a crack in the wing. We were to divert to the nearest land mass. Greenland.

It took a while to sink in. Could we land safely with a damaged wing? I guessed we probably couldn't. As I stowed the cannisters and the trolleys, making sure none would shoot out and whack my head, I went through the emergency evacuation drill, then thought how stupid I'd been to give up smoking. If I was going to die in the next few hours why had I bothered trying to be healthy, slimmer, less outrageous? I wondered how many complementary peanuts I had handed out, how many hot towels, how many exits I'd encouraged the familiarisation thereof. I wondered what they would say at my funeral and how people who really knew me would lament I had so much more life to come, how I hadn't yet arrived fully at what I was good at. What a fool I was to believe I could prolong my life when my imminent demise must've been written in the stars. I thought of Mum, back home, with her firm belief in fate, but not this kind of fate, blind to the fact her daughter would soon perish. I wished I'd told her I loved her, but she didn't like these words. She believed it was shown through action, all the many packed lunches she'd made, the cups of tea, the endless cakes and tucking into bed. I wanted words from her mouth, soap opera style, as if it would underscore it and set it in stone. I should have said them anyway, forced them at her in a text via satellite.

Everything was silent apart from the low murmur of the engines. The passengers had been warned there was a technical fault with the plane. From where I was sitting, I couldn't see any faces, but I could sense the collective stillness, quiet, like a praying congregation. I expected panic, screaming, clambering over one another like the scene with the singing nun in the film *Airplane*.

It was then that the purser's interphone rang. She took the call, stood, then came over close.

'It's all okay,' she said, 'we can carry on with the service. It's not serious. You can go up to the flight deck and see the window if you like?'

'The window?'

'Yes, the splintered window on the flight deck. In front of the first officer. There's eight layers to the glass, so it's quite safe to carry on to JFK.'

'Oh,' I said, 'I thought you'd said win ...'

The purser waited for me to finish, but I kept the 'g' in my mouth. To admit it would mean I would have to say so much more about how things were getting out of control.

'Of course, the window,' I said.

I had misheard. It was not the first time, but the consultant had confirmed my hearing was fine. Afterwards, he'd asked whether I was happy, which was a strange question for an ear doctor. He said we don't hear sometimes if we're disengaged, and this can present as hearing loss.

By the flight deck door, I rubbed the goosebumps on my arm. In the middle of the night, the flight always turned cold. Then I knocked three times and faced the spy-hole so they would know I was crew. Beneath this uniform was my body, the body I was born with which had housed me for all these years. Thumping conduits of blood and electricity were keeping me alive. Somewhere within all this skin was something called 'me', but I wasn't sure what this was.

3

When the captain opened the door, I softened my eyes into a hello. There it was, the right-hand window, shattered yet held in a crash of crisscrossing lines; the universe outside might not exist.

CHAPTER 1

Acceptable Reasons
For Late Arrival

London

There was a specific moment I can chart as to when things started to go awry. My cheek was pressed to the lounge carpet at number forty-seven and Mum was bent over, her heels popping out of her slippers, consumed in what I thought was a narrow mesh of living: obsessing over small domestic problems, like dust or wiping skirting boards, or defrosting freezer compartments. Yet I worried how I still needed her in a way I couldn't specify. Now at twenty-five I was not allowed to be a child, I was an adult living back at home, and the scales no longer tipped in my favour.

'There,' she said, shifting the coffee table over an inch. 'Meet the new lounge.'

Lifting my head, I saw the latest configuration *had*

given the room a lift. But the bay window above, once so cinematic, now began at my head and ended at my toes. My sister's freedom car, ready to whisk us off from Dad at any point, was no longer parked outside. This street was too small, too familiar. Back here in Penge I was a failure, cleaning my old secondary school toilets for cash. The girls stuck their used sanitary towels, face out, on the cubicle walls. Maybe this was modern witchcraft, or a fingers up to authority, whatever, it was certainly dismissive of the person cleaning up.

'Help me move the sofa. See if there's any grain of rice type things,' Mum said, like I would join in. 'That's evidence they're back.'

'Don't moths have stomachs and nervous systems?' I said. 'You shouldn't be killing . . .'

'Isn't there enough going on, without you . . .?' Mum said.

'You've hoovered once, so . . .' I said, splaying my fingers at the room.

'God, you sound like your father. I'm double-checking.' Mum's cheeks had gone red.

'I'm not Dad,' I said, like I was thirteen. Her likening me to him was the last thing I wanted. I didn't have a drink problem. Plus, I had friends. Lots. My brain fired up after a pint or three, I danced and flashed and never got nasty.

While I was in Australia trying to make it as a performance artist, a horde of gold moths had been spotted here in the carpets, their larval pupas stuck behind the curtains. This was the big news she'd written in her letter, nothing more personal. If it'd been a metaphor for her dissatisfaction with Dad, I would've understood – how moths were drawn to fake light, believing it was the radiance of the moon – but we weren't a family who used metaphors.

After a long inspection she put the hoover attachment down. She rubbed her forehead, and from her sigh, I knew the pressure of me living back home was difficult. And Dad, she still chose him after all he'd done to us. Before I'd left for art college, I'd painted him naked and blue, strung up by a noose. Then I'd propped the picture above my bedroom door, trying to force the evil pull of the booze away. When he'd brought me a cup of tea the next morning, he'd walked in under the painting, not seeing it balanced on the doorframe. I'd realised the man I carried in my head from the night times was not the soft man sat on my bed in the morning. Because I loved him when he wasn't drunk, I destroyed the painting as fast as possible.

'Now, why don't you give the airline a call?' Mum said. 'I think it would do you good, see more of this world while getting paid for it.' She held out her hand to pull me up. 'You never know . . .I could even join you. Be a "cling-on",' she said, twitching her head in a weird way.

Motioning me over, together we slid the table in front of the drinks cupboard under the record player. This was the latest attempt at curbing Dad's drinking; the other week he'd stumbled over an open water works hole and ripped his best work trousers.

'It's not me, cabin crew. Tea, coffee, tea, coffee,' I said, moving my hands like a robot.

'Why shouldn't it be you? There are worse ways to make a living. You are always saving to go off travelling. And the art . . .well, it's not too late to retrain. I would think it would be good for you.'

My eyes darted down at the coffee table, feeling the shame. The first person in my family to study at university and I couldn't hack it now I'd left. All those years finding my wings: film-making, photography, nudity, wig-wearing, impersonations of Julie Andrews, following my gut, feeling my glow; I'd believed I was on the brink of becoming something big. Dad had suggested I study graphic design, so I would be sure to land a job, but that was selling out. When I left Cardiff Art School, I had a show at the Institute of Contemporary Arts and thought this was the beginning. Then I'd entered The World's First Miss Lesbian Beauty Contest held at the Café de Paris, thinking this was my way into my extraordinary future. When nothing happened, I couldn't work out how or why I should make art. So my sister got me a job at Barclays bank in Streatham, processing cheques with nothing but a portable radio to keep me human. Cellulite formed on the backs of my thighs, reminding me of cauliflower and rot. I'd read somewhere how you shouldn't let a job define who you were, but I couldn't work out how not to.

'You see, love,' Mum said, picking up the furniture polish, then performing a wipe round the television screen. 'Life is all about having to do things you don't want to.'

Her philosophy was threadbare, so poor it made me want to scream. I was not going to turn out like this, caught in a room, searching for moths. Only last week, after a particularly silent standoff with Dad, she'd disappeared. Later, when she returned, she confided she'd left home only to go on the 227 to Bromley and back. Twice, she said, and the driver hadn't charged her for the second journey which became the golden lining to the story. She'd have stayed out longer, she said, if it'd been Thursday late-night shopping.

'So, anyhow, I got you the airline phone number from Juan up the road.' She pronounced 'Ju-an' carefully, enjoying the foreign quality dance over her tongue. 'He loves it.

Do you know he was in a hot tub in Miami last week? Took his mum to Kenya. She sat on an elephant.'

'Why are you telling me this?' I blurted. Too sharp.

She turned, flushed-face. 'You should focus on being like my side of the family. The light side.'

'Can I go now?' She nodded, and I noticed there was a roll of dust on her sleeve. As I went to pick it off, she stepped back. To the outside eye no one would notice this flinching, but to me it was everything. Since I'd told her I didn't like men, how I had never liked them in *that* way, there had been no more touching. I hoped I was imagining it, but whatever the reason, she was uncomfortable. I feared she believed if I held her too intensely, it was because I wanted her in a lesbian way.

The telephone number for the airline was in the hall. I grabbed it then took the stairs to Mum and Dad's bedroom, sinking onto Dad's side where I studied the marbled blood stains on his pillow. Last year's book on cricket scores sat closed on the table next to the telephone. I opened the pot where he stored his false teeth. He'd worn them since he was forty, losing his real ones early because he was too scared to visit the dentist. The container was empty; he was down the pub. It was a Saturday, and Mum allowed him to have lunchtime drinks on Saturdays. Along with Mondays, Wednesdays, and Fridays after dinner, she kept him on a tight schedule. The official line was his diabetes. Still, I found the pot intriguing, as if it were a way to get closer to him. I examined the dull shine in the plastic bowl. It smelt of unchanged pedal bins.

Picking up the phone, I smoothed the crumpled paper over my knee. Baulking at Mum's peach curtains, I pictured how many women were rearranging rooms right now across

London, then multiplied this. I would not become another one. I would be strident. Taking in a deep breath, I dialled the number. It rang immediately, then clicked to a plucky operatic harp. I recognised the tune from the TV ad where people of different nationalities were reunited for a wedding in Japan. I wanted to be the kind of person who had friends in Tokyo and drank Martinis on rooftops in Manhattan.

When the call reached a human voice, I jumped, spurting out, 'hello?'

The gap which followed made me realise it was a recording. The office was now closed and would reopen on Monday morning.

Replacing the receiver, I felt relief. Mum had got it wrong about me being right for the job, of course. An air hostess was never going to make me into me. Everyone knew parents had the worst ideas for their offspring. So far I'd made it to my mid-twenties without having one hair-style Mum liked. I certainly would not call back on Monday because I would've figured things out by then. That afternoon I would go to the library and read through the back copies of *National Geographic*. There would be broadsheets with job pages hanging off wooden poles and recent copies of *Lonely Planet*. Then I would go out with the L Gang to a gay bar in Brixton. My true purpose would find me if only I got out and into the breadth of life. I would just have to save up by working in rubbish jobs a bit longer, then I could get to Mexico. There the cost of living was cheap; artists had settled in the south since the sixties. Avocados grew on trees. I would drink quality tequila, and dress all in white, and if I got there by December, arrive in time to celebrate the Night of the Radishes.

*

Dressed in a pink satin blouse tucked into a charcoal-grey pencil skirt, I listened to the foreign tube names announcing themselves west out of London: Barons Court, Hammersmith, Osterley, Hounslow. Between each stop I made sure there were no smudges to my black eye-pencil, opening and closing the information pack, examining the sides of my shoes. Borrowed from Mum, the little court heel was repulsive: the uniform of church-goers, or shoes you might be fitted in for your own funeral, if no one knew you.

Arriving at Hatton Cross I clutched the airline folder and took the stairs to the ticket hall. The air outside smelt of car fumes and my tights had slipped down between my legs. I would only get to yank them up once I found a toilet. Being nearly six foot tall I'd spent years hitching up one thing or another, pulling waistbands lower, trying to fit in. I was not comfortable in these clothes. I used to be confident, a spontaneous woman who wore hobnail boots and flowing maternity dresses to thwart the male gaze, a kind of anti-uniform of my own.

I found the stop for the transfer bus. The sky was crossed with contrails. Soon enough a minibus arrived with a sign on the dashboard, 'Meadowbank'. On board were women in smart office attire reading the information pack. As I boarded, practising psychic Morse code, I tried to connect with the rigid mousse-haired woman at the front. *I feel as nervous as you, this is risky,* I sent over to her. But she did not pick up.

The bus took a series of winding roads circumnavigating the airport until we pulled up outside an ugly brown building with reflective windows. Through a set of automatic doors, I followed the sign for 'INTERVIEW CANDIDATES: Stage One' and entered a room full of dipped heads and already-breathed air. The majority were women in dresses and short matching jackets. A couple wore trouser suits with wheelie suitcases parked by their knees. One woman stood out because of her tight stone-washed jeans and low-cut top, her cleavage pressed into a vertical line. Was this what the airline wanted? This out-dated barmaid look?

I chastised myself for putting the woman down, then searched about the room for clues. That morning I'd brushed my blonde bob into a side parting and tucked it behind my ears, feminine but to the informed eye, an edge of otherness. Most of the women around me had their hair held back in tight shiny buns, like ringed doughnuts. A high percentage were stick thin, with bony knees jutting from the hem of their skirts. One of the questions on the form was about your weight, and I'd got on the scales then subtracted ten pounds. For days I'd eaten cream cheese triangles, diet crackers, grapes. I'd switched lager for white wine, but still hadn't dropped more than a couple of pounds.

I spotted an empty seat next to an older woman dressed in a navy trouser suit and a white lace-collared blouse. Her hair was cropped in a pixie cut which gave me a flutter of hope. As I sat down, I nodded, careful not to be too over-enthusiastic.

'Here we are then. The big interview,' the woman said, moving her wheelie bag.

'Yep,' I said.

'Brenda, hi.' The woman put out her hand. She had an Australian accent.

'Karen,' I said, cringing at my name, how unlike me it still felt. I shook her fingers loosely.

'How far have you come?' she said.

'What year do you want me to start?' I said, noticing her accent had already slipped into mine.

'No, I meant travelled in from.'

'Oh, South London,' I said. 'You?'

'Flew in from Brisbane yesterday.'

'For this?'

'Yeah,' she said. 'It's my dream to fly again. Years ago, I worked for Qantas, but I left when I got married. Then I got divorced from the prick, usual story. I made it through round one for Air New Zealand, never went any further though. You tried other airlines?'

'No, this is my first,' I said, feeling ashamed for applying when I didn't really want it, when the job clearly mattered so much to her.

'You don't sound like a Londoner.'

'I lived abroad for a while,' I said. 'I accidentally pick up people's accents. I can't help it. My mum does it too. I guess you could say we're a family of impersonators.'

'You'll get on fine in this job then,' Brenda laughed. 'Theatrical. You got a boyfriend?'

'No ... I've, I'm ...' I breathed in, weighing up whether to say or not. I decided against it.

'Sure,' Brenda said, eyeing me. I noticed my thumb pressing into my arm fat, so released it.

'Doesn't make us less of a woman,' I said, brightly. 'Single-dom.'

I heard my voice do that annoying thing, the one where I made a ditzy-light impression of myself to make someone else feel more comfortable. As I shifted in my seat I could tell Brenda's familiarity had dropped. So we sat in silence, me sifting through my notes, re-reading my CV, checking the exaggerated parts, while Brenda wound her ring round her smallest finger. Then in the corner, over Brenda's shoulder, a cheese plant caught my eye. I studied the brown earth in the pot, the wide leaves. The plant was perfect for bugs, the listening kind. Perhaps the airline recorded us in the interview room, perhaps they were watching me right now examining the hyperreal shine of those leaves?

Soon a woman in the airline uniform invited us into the adjoining room. I queued a few people away from Brenda, just so she didn't think I was obsessed with her. Through the folded-back partition were chairs fitted with flap-tables. WELCOME! was projected on a white screen. I found a seat three along from Brenda and tried to get my table to lie flat over my knees. The woman next to me gave me a sympathetic smile as I uncrossed my legs.

The training staff introduced themselves: Jenny, chignon, had flown for twenty-six years before moving to training. She missed the shopping 'down route' but loved being home to tuck her children into bed at night. Brian, softly spoken, attractive though boss-eyed, expanded on the expression 'down route', explaining that it was a phrase for where crew stayed in 'super, five-star hotels'. The mention of hotels made me lean forward. Both Jenny and Brian sounded suspiciously chirpy. Most people I'd met in the world of work carried an air of just about getting through it. Brian told us how he had flown long-haul from Heathrow for eight years, but now had a serious injury so he was grounded. He looked fit enough and I suspected there was a different story beneath the acceptable one.

Brian pressed play on a video where a radiant, cheerful crew walked across an airport tarmac. In the distance was the smooth white underbelly of a plane. The captain was mid-fifties with impeccable grooming. He smiled proudly

14

at his crew, the stewardesses and the one good-looking steward. When it finished Jenny changed the slide: 'Interview Process'. She ran her eye over us, clasping her hands together.

'Although we are recruiting vast numbers,' she said, 'some candidates will not succeed. Do remember you can always re-apply, as occasionally it takes two, three, sometimes four attempts before being accepted. In a recent poll taken by UK job seekers, the career most sought after, just below surgeon, pilot, and TV personality, was cabin crew. It isn't just any job, it's an extremely desirable job. It's a way of life.'

I searched about the room. Brenda had thrust her chin forward making a claim on her potential future. So I pulled back my shoulders, pressed my toes into the carpet tiles, and decided I was going to be a success. Even if I hadn't wanted it at first, I kind of did now. I wasn't going to fail at something I didn't really want, because wouldn't it be somehow worse than failing at something I did want?

The day splintered into a series of interviews. Brenda disappeared into a group for the maths and English test while I was sent for a language test. I managed the twenty-minute conversation I'd rehearsed about my life in French, which sounded more interesting than in English, but my cheeks reddened when the woman began something called *'compréhension culturelle'*.

The second interview was with a duo consisting of Jenny, whose legs were bronzed and buffed up like conkers, and a man with sunglass patches around his eyes. From behind the desk they asked questions such as, how would I feel being away from home for lengthy periods? What was good customer service? Tell us about a time when you had to influence someone to your way of thinking?

I had prepared a few scenarios, mainly based on true experiences (they'd listed topics to think about in the pre-interview pack), so I told them the story of when I worked in a café in Sydney. A particularly drunk man (I left out he was gay, in case they thought I was homophobic – though it was intrinsic to the story) had become annoyed when I refused to serve him more alcohol. First, I'd tried humour, then when he refused to take no for an answer, he called me 'a stupid bitch' and demanded to be served by 'one of the boys'. I said he could have one last gin and tonic and, using Mum's trick, wiped the rim of the glass with an alcohol-soaked tissue. Watching as he'd drunk down the tonic and ice, he was none the wiser. All he could smell was gin.

'Do you think that was a satisfying outcome?' Jenny said. 'Being duped?'

'Well, it certainly stopped the anger,' I said, then Jenny wrote for a long time, her hand brushing across the paper in spurts everyone could hear.

The penultimate part of the day was the 'teamwork' exercise. We were split into groups of eight, then told to sit on the floor in a circle. It was difficult to find a suitable position with my skirt being as it was, but I found a comfortable side-turn with my knees.

Brian was the leader, which I was pleased about, because he came across as more lenient than Jenny. 'Now, I want you to imagine you've crash landed on a desert island,' he explained. 'Here are two boxes. In this one you'll find ten items. The other is empty. Now, *together in a team*, and *listening to one another,* choose the most important item to keep for your group's survival. And then, put that *one item* into the empty box. You have three minutes to work this out, *by talking with one another.* So, ready, steady, go!'

The group rushed forward onto the carpet and began pulling out objects: a lighter, water filter, first-aid kit, adult lifejacket, a doll-baby in a lifejacket, saucepan, sun-tan lotion, mirror, wine bottle, and a survival manual. The others announced the objects out loud, and I realised I was being inactive, so I pushed my way into the circle. Grabbing hold of the lighter, I waited to work out why this could be important.

'We should take the saucepan!' a French woman shouted, holding it in the air, waiting for a glance from Brian.

'Surely save the baby?' another woman said.

'It's not real,' I said. 'It could be a hoax.'

'It is real,' the woman said, cradling it.

'What about the lighter? For fire?' I said, knowing fire was once intrinsic to cavemen.

'No, we'll need something to cook in,' the French woman said. 'Or we shall die.'

Everyone started talking over each other, the noise becoming frenzied.

'Sun-tan cream. Burns are deadly!'

'Water filter, we can live without food, but not water.'

'No, the mirror, to reflect the sun into a signal. To be saved by passing aircraft!'

'If we have a lighter, we can cook food and also boil water,' I pointed out.

'Let's take a vote,' someone shouted, but Brian called time and the French woman threw the saucepan in the box. I scanned her face, feeling revulsion towards her lack of negotiation. I knew it then, she would save herself above all others and as I watched Brian writing on his pad, I was sure she wouldn't make it through the process.

It was all over. As we filed back into the classroom, we

didn't find out what the correct object was for survival. I thought maybe this was the point – there was no right or wrong answer – continued existence could be the only aim. Though as time passed, I was unsure whether my approach was any better than the French woman's.

At the end of the day, I joined the queue to be weighed. I hadn't eaten or drunk anything since breakfast and felt far away from my body. Like everyone else I took off my shoes and placed them against the wall. As we waited, I inspected their feet with their gnarls and peculiar bones. Then I noticed the crevices between the women's toes. So intimate, I thought, they appeared like a series of small cleavages all lined up.

When Brian called my name, I entered the room and watched as the woman in front got off the stand. The scales were digital with a black rubber cover. As I stepped on, I made sure a fraction of my heels were slightly off the back.

'Move a little forward please,' Brian said. 'You're, ah, twelve stone two.'

Pinned to the wall was a colour chart with acceptable height to weight ratios. I was a stone over what I'd said I was. According to the chart I was in the purple zone, the colour of thrombosis. I wished I could've taken off my clothes. The skirt and blouse would probably weigh three pounds alone. I should've cut my hair short, swapped toast for apples, wine for water. I would've if I'd wanted this job as much as Brenda. I wanted to ask Brian if this meant I was discounted. Instead, I decided I should try to befriend him by telling him I'd slept with women. The way he groomed his hair, he was surely gay. If he knew, he might grant me special dispensation. But how could I slip this information casually into the situation?

He wrote my weight into his folder.

'Thanks,' he said.

'Thank *you*,' I said, forcing humour.

No reaction, not even an eyebrow flicker.

'You know . . .' I began.

'Next,' he said, pointing for the woman behind to step forward. 'And make sure you stand in the centre of the scales please.'

Days and weeks went by with something plummeting, pulling me down, as if my newly imagined future was departing without me. Because I'd now envisioned myself as cabin crew, the idea had formed roots. I'd recalled things, reasons to help the idea fit, like how as a girl after our first Spanish holiday abroad, a stewardess had smiled right at me, making me wriggle. Like an arrow charged with love, I had felt seen. After that I had wanted a tray table in my bedroom, and I'd tucked the salt and pepper sachets in the drawer of my felt jewellery box.

Every night after work I drank away the evenings. There was always someone to go out with. At weekends I met the L Gang and talked through art project ideas. I always had something on the boil, but then we'd get drunk, and it wouldn't matter anymore.

It was early August when the letter arrived. With my eyes screwed into pinholes in my bedroom, I ripped open the envelope, bracing myself. One word immediately lifted up from the second paragraph: *Congratulations*. They were offering me the role of cabin crew based at London Gatwick, Worldwide Fleet. I read it over and over to make sure the words didn't rearrange themselves. Sure, the job was dependent on passing an HIV, hearing and sight test, as well as the six-week training course. There was no mention of wages anywhere, but I'd lived on a student loan and overdraft before and made it work. Besides, this was good news for Mum. The static quality of the previous months were about to be recharged by this unexpected right turn.

That evening, to celebrate, Mum cooked lamb chops with roast potatoes and garlic bread. As a special occasion it would be served out on the patio. She got out the placemats, and folded paper serviettes into fans. I blow-dried my hair and put on bright lipstick before taking a seat, pretending it was an al fresco restaurant. The small lawn was the Mediterranean. A bottle of white wine appeared from the fridge and then Dad arrived with his curls combed flat, a bottle of red tucked under his arm.

Mum brought out the plates. 'Hot, hot, hot!'

As we started to eat, Tammy Dog arrived on the back-door step, her filmy cataracts veiling her eyes. She rarely moved from her bed these days, but it was a rare warm summer's evening, and we were together. As she waited, her eyelashes lowering as she caught the scent of chops, her tail jerked in a short wag, in an echo of her full wagging years.

The golden sunset was setting over next door's roof shooting out wild pinks and oranges. Surprisingly, it turned into the rarest of jovial dinners. I drank the white wine and Dad his bottle of red. After a while, I felt we were all adults, becoming friends even, rather than a family.

'So, remind me, where did you and Dad meet?' I said.

'The Christmas party,' Mum said. 'I walked into the men's by mistake.'

Dad laughed, knowing the anecdote. I had also heard it before, all two sentences of it.

'What was it like for you?' I said.

'The party?' Mum said.

'No, life back then?'

Dad cleared his throat, swivelled his bottle round to read the label as if it held crucial information.

'I liked it,' he said. Picking up his glass, he drank it down in one. Then he pressed both sets of his fingers on the edge of the table, about to stand. Mum's eyes lowered him back down to his chair.

'What was he like, I mean, what were you like back then?'

'Funny,' Mum said. 'Liked an adventure.'

'Oh yes, you spent your national service in Cyprus?' I said.

'Yes, he did. Didn't you Jeff?'

' . . .'

'What do you remember?' I asked. 'It must have been weird, after the war had ended. Like a holiday?'

He leant back and brushed something off the table. Hundreds of different-sized moles dotted his arms. Galaxies, I thought. The body was a universe.

'Did you always want to work in car insurance, Dad?'

'What's this, bloody Mastermind?'

'Jeff!'

'I would have had the snip if I knew . . .' Dad scraped back his chair, then took the steps up into the kitchen.

'What was that he said . . .?'

Mum shook her head. 'He doesn't mean it. It's just his work, you know.'

No, I didn't know how work could make someone so mean. Surely he could change jobs if it was so bad? Now I had a proper job, I saw how easy it was to pass interviews.

'We're alright, aren't we?' Mum said, her eyes

red-rimmed. She was so beautiful, even with the outdated perm. 'You'll be okay.'

With Dad gone, I finished my wine and waited for pudding. A hefty blue folder sat upstairs on my old school desk with 'Pre-Work Training' printed on the front. They suggested we learn every airport code across the globe. Some were obvious – JFK (John F Kennedy) (SIN) Singapore but some didn't make sense – EZE (Buenos Aires) or MCO (Orlando). From the back room I had taken Dad's old atlas, along with his pocketbook on British birds and Mum's medical dictionary. To learn about the world, I'd decided to tackle it by placing a stick-it note with the code written over every destination. Perhaps even make a collage.

From above I heard the toilet flush and water gush down the pipes. After a few minutes I was surprised to see Dad return with two large brandies in the special crystal glasses. Mum, our usual intermediary, got up and went into the kitchen. Then it was just Dad and me, and I kept my eyes averted as he sat down, nervous in case he said anything hurtful again.

'Cognac *con hielo*,' he announced. I smiled, raising the glass in a half-cheers, remembering how he'd taught me to say this to the Spanish bartender when I was nine or ten. Back then I'd pictured the word '*hielo*' as the word 'yellow'. *Brandy and yellow*, I'd thought as I carried it over to his sun lounger, proud to be his personal waitress. As a reward he allowed me a crème de menthe, which glinted like emerald poison.

'Ew, that's strong,' I said, feeling the burn.

'It's quality.'

Mum switched on the radio, then turned it up. She started to sing along in that high-pitched voice she used for

Christmas carols. *Every now and then I'll get a little bit restless.*
She clattered the plates on the drying rack, and I got the
hint about the drinking. The choice, as always, was mine:
Dad or her. Be good like her or bad like him. I wanted both
and to be neither of them.

By the way he rested in his patio chair I could tell he was
pleased I was drinking the brandy. We were less uncomfortable now the bridge was here. Maybe nothing could
hurt now. I lifted my glass: once like creosote, it tasted of
grapefruit.

'Smells of the sun,' he said, examining his brandy up
against the falling sky.

'Fruity,' I added.

At this moment the urge came. I wanted to get really
drunk. Out of it. Free from the weight of my body and
the confines of my clothes. I guessed he did too because
he swallowed fast. Once his glass was drained, he got up,
nipped a head off Mum's lavender, then shot it over next
door's fence. I went and stood by Mum, hoping for a hug,
and she flicked some suds at me from the washing bowl to
make me laugh. He was gone a while, but when he came
back I was sat back outside and he was with the Brandy
bottle.

'So what did you enjoy so much about playing cricket?' I
said, the drink opening up a topic he'd talk about. I wished
I could light a cigarette, but it'd never felt right to do so
at home.

He mused a while, circling his glass.

'The camaraderie.'

'You had lots of friends then, at the club?'

'Not what I'd call friends exactly.'

Now one of those solid gaps.

'I was thinking the other day, if you had a favourite type of bird?' I said. 'If you had to choose one . . .?'

'Why do you want to know?' he said, in a civilised tone. I pushed my glass towards him a fraction and he poured me a drop.

'If it were a choice, between life and death . . .? Which bird, Dad?'

I'd called him Dad, a strike at intimacy and he'd felt it. Mum turned opening a cupboard, one ear always out for danger in case she needed to step in. Not that she ever could, it being all atmospheres and subtexts rather than actual physical happenings. She carried on drying the dishes and I drank a sip down, feeling my engines start to rev. As long as we stayed here, in this spot, Mum couldn't say anything about the drink, but she was there just in case. Dad knew this too. Safety in numbers. It was a dangerous communion of sorts.

Then he sighed in a way which demonstrated he'd been holding his breath.

'Long-tailed tit, I suppose,' he said, giving in.

That was enough for me and so the sun lowered in the distance. There was no talk of the job, my possible joy-filled adventurous future. No talk of anything much, just us and our insides lifting off on fire surrounded by the crazy-paving.

On the final day of the training course, from an initial class of twenty, only fifteen of us were left. One trainee had been sent home because she couldn't shout loud enough during an emergency door drill and the others had just caved under the pressure.

We were led into a small room full of orange jumpsuits

which smelt of gym changing rooms. I was handed a large men's size and once we'd changed, we queued up along a metal staircase, the grating harsh on our bare feet. A mock fuselage of a Boeing 747 towered above us. At around sixty feet high the upper-deck slide dropped down almost vertically. In order to use the slide, you had to take a running jump, then lift your knees with your arms crossed, fingers gripping your collar so as not to cut open your palms. Once descended, your boiler suit would catch the base of the slide and propel you onto your feet to start you running.

I had no memory of how, or if I'd ever been brave. The boldest thing I'd done so far was change my name to 'Tom' at art college. People had used it without question and for a while I'd been free to explore whoever this was. But now, here I was, the 'Karen' on my name badge, suddenly realising I was afraid of heights, realising I hadn't thought any of this through since I believed I would be carried in an aircraft, not ever facing a physical and willing descent.

One, two, three . . . My knees began to twitch and wobble. I counted to five. Pressing the railing between my fingers, I knew I had to jump. So, for the very first time consciously, I stopped thinking and ran, leaping while lifting my knees in the vast space, then dropping into sheer chance.

Air stuffed the open cave of my mouth. The gagging shocked me – how easy it was to become suffocated by something as everyday as air! Before I knew it, the Velcro patch at the base of the slide caught my jumpsuit, yanked my knickers into a thong, then threw me onto my feet. How solid the ground was as my right ankle wrenched over. Still, I corrected my balance then couldn't stop running. I was in a state of thrust, uncontrolled, until I punched into the blue crash mat and found myself on the floor. I stood up at once, ignoring the pain in my ankle. If I showed any weakness I would have to come back and repeat the jump. Composing myself, I strode over casually to the group, foot throbbing. The others, all pink and high, enthused how they'd like to do the jump again. I grinned, thinking how they were all insane, while nodding along with a fake enthusiasm.

I pictured the curved shoulders of a bottle of wine and a cigarette. Maybe invite everyone round for a celebratory cheers. It was eleven in the morning, and we still had the medical exams that afternoon. We were being put up at the Hilton near the perimeter fence. My room had a view of the control tower, and I could make out heads moving behind the glass. I calculated we would be back by six. I'd pick up a bottle and thanks to completing my medical training, R.I.C.E, knew to rest, ice my ankle, compress and elevate it above my head.

For the rest of that last day, each time the trainers came into view, casually watching over us during lunch in the canteen, or passing by us smoking outside, I hid my swollen ankle behind suitable furniture. I pretended to be pain-free, learning fast how the authentic me could remain safely behind a presentable host who also happened to be me. This should have signalled danger, this splitting, this doubling, but it was ever so everyday to me.

CHAPTER 2

Lift Off

LGW – NBO – LGW

As the train pulled into Gatwick, commuters stared intently at my uniform and my face as if I were a puzzle they wanted to work out. When a man offered to help me with my case onto the platform, I said I was fine, while he placed his hand on the handle. My mother's world, one where women didn't carry suitcases, swayed close behind me. In the end, I let him lift it; I was now part of an airline, I couldn't quibble over an outdated idea of chivalry. I decided not to say 'no' on my first day.

As people sped along the platform, a few slowed to let me by. I walked briskly towards the escalator, feeling like I was starring in my own documentary. All the time I sensed the eyes on me. John Berger's book *Ways of Seeing* sprang to mind, how 'men look, and women watch themselves being looked at. Men act, women appear.' Since I'd read this,

I'd tried to stop seeing myself through the lens of others. Molested in the street at the age of eleven, the breast-grab had shaken me into a girl with a before-body and after-body, of dreamy then awake. I wanted to walk along the street in my own kind of female camera, not realising myself from outside in, but inside out.

Determined to have control – I couldn't do anything about the uniform hat – I decided to be in charge of the lift. So, as the public filed in, I stood to the side making sure it was my hand which was nearest the over-sized DEPARTURES button. While they slotted their sizes into the cramped space, one woman studied the yellow CREW label on my suitcase, and I felt a quiver at what lay ahead.

From the terminal, I took the bus to the crew report centre. To research my trip to Nairobi I'd watched the video *Out of Africa* with Mum. Set in Kenya, Meryl Streep played the colonialist author Karen Blixen, whose husband had bought a coffee plantation. She joined him in Nairobi where he'd had an affair, then given her syphilis. To this day there was a part of Nairobi called 'Karen' which seemed significant and made me wonder whether there was a divine plan. When the film ended, Mum passed the tissue box and I wrote down four words: pen, plane, poetry, fire, which formed the basic plot of the film. I'd slipped this into my pocket as a potential talisman.

The crew report centre was a low modernist block next to the derelict Freddie Laker building. I showed my pass and headed towards the desk to collect the company Diners Card. I read the red safety notices then sat with a coffee in Wingtips café, making bite marks in the polystyrene cup. The runway was on view with planes lining up, nose to tail, and I thought how organised the world was, convincing myself that the dishevelled, anything goes world of performance art wasn't so great after all.

When it was time, I checked my name badge was straight, and tights snag free at the back. Earlier Mum had stood by the front door, her eyes wide as she swept the lint roller over the sleeves of my uniform jacket.

'I'm so proud of you,' she said. 'That straw hat suits you so well.' And although I tried hard not to, her all too effusive approval at this new life had niggled me all the way to the station.

Upon opening the door to briefing room number two, I was faced with seventeen sky-blue chairs arranged in a horseshoe. I took a seat opposite the entrance, then decided it was too confrontational to face the crew as they came in, so moved towards the lone desk at the front. I guessed the cabin service director (CSD) would sit here, and I didn't want to appear like teacher's pet, so I settled on a neutral seat with eight chairs either side.

As the crew entered, they all recognised one another like old friends. The CSD, Susan Harding, entered the room with a perfumey walk, plonking her gaping handbag open onto the table. A series of pens were clipped in the front pocket. The room hushed as she handed round the briefing sheets. When it was my turn, her blue eyes fixed on me, and she took extra time and something deep inside squirmed. I was still learning how sexual excitement and nerves chimed near identical notes. Sometimes I even confused a full bladder with being stirred up. Her skirt hung loosely from her hips and her arms were tanned and thin, her blonde hair pulled into a cliff-shape. She was possibly over fifty, and still so beautiful.

'Good afternoon,' Susan said, her voice clear and strong.

'Now, we all know today's flight to Nairobi is monumental. I'm sorry to say, but it will go down in history as the last flight where passengers can legally smoke.'

'The beginning of the end,' a stewardess shook her red frizz of hair.

'The last gasp,' a Nordic looking steward added.

'Quite so,' Susan laughed, softening. 'The end of an era. But we will make this one to remember.'

Cheers came from two mahogany-tanned stewards, who I checked over for gay signs.

'Any new entrants?'

'Yes,' I said, raising my hand. There was no applause, just a series of head turns.

'Welcome,' Susan said. 'The purser in economy today is Peter, and he will look after you.' A steward with a gelled black fringe nodded, smiling a string of white teeth.

We all chose our positions in the different classes and wrote down each crew member's number beside their name. As I was the newest and least senior, I was number sixteen, 'mums and babies' in charge of families and wheel-chair passengers.

On boarding I showed a woman carrying an infant to her seat by the bulkhead at the front of economy. From the special stowage, I fetched her an orange extension seatbelt, fastening it around the baby, getting a nudge of its warm doughy stomach. I then showed the mother how this looped onto her own seatbelt. The baby stared up and I thought how later I should let Peter see me cradle it, letting the mother go to the toilet, so it could go on my assessment. As I walked back towards the door for boarding, I realised how professional I'd been not to mention what the belt was really for: how in the event of landing on water, she would yank the drowning baby back towards her with the strap, potentially saving its life.

Along the jetty were six wheelchair passengers lined up, each with a ground staff member. The last was a middle-aged woman in large sunglasses and long red pleated skirt. She was blind, so during the dinner service I would guide her through the tray using the clock-method. Holding her hand, we'd locate her starter at three o'clock, the hot meal at six, desert across at nine and cheese and biscuits just before midnight. Depending on who made up the tray, the trainers said the coffee cup would either be at 1am or 11pm. Time moved differently in this job, I noted.

As soon as I'd completed my number sixteen duties, Peter asked me to help boarding in business class. So I stood in the leg room of an empty cradle seat, running my hand over the thatched material, enjoying my proximity to the luxury. Soon, a white-haired woman dressed in linen stood close, forcing me to turn. Studying the locker numbers, she showed me her boarding pass while giving off an air of disdain. Stood behind was her husband in a Panama hat. They settled into 12J and 12K, then asked me to lift their Louis Vuitton bag in the overhead locker. It weighed nearly nothing.

Before long, a man in African dress arrived with a woman in a head wrap of orange and gold. Their children were smartly dressed, the girls with frilly ankle socks, and the boy in a suit and tie. Between them they had ten pieces of bulky carry-on luggage.

The man began piling the bags into the overhead lockers. The white-haired woman appeared anxious as she watched him. When she began discussing it with her husband, I tried to hear what they were saying, but the boarding music drowned out their whispers.

'Miss?' 12J beckoned me over. 'Our locker, above us – that gentleman has put his bags in with ours.'

I peered into the container, then nodded. 'Yes?'

'I'm afraid he has used *our* space,' 12J said. 'Could you ask him to move his bags out?'

'Sorry, madam ...' I said. 'Do you have more luggage which needs to go up?'

'No, no, we don't. That's not the point. It's our room, isn't it?'

Her husband leant over, 'We paid for it.' But he was less involved than the wife.

'Well ...' I paused, keeping my face in what I hoped was neutral.

'It's part of our ticket,' 12K said. 'So, the whole area belongs to us.'

'The overhead lockers are ...' I said. 'The space is free for everyone to use, madam.'

This hadn't been in the training, this odd nit-picking about lockers and how far the price of a ticket stretched. I wondered if there was a psychological element to this, how the space above one's head could actually mean headspace.

Way down the plane, Peter was stood in the aisle examining a printout. I hoped he would come and help me, but I knew it was my job to sort it out. We'd been instructed to humanise irate passengers by pretending they were members of our own family. So I thought of Mum and got down on one knee to be at eye level. The carpet prickled as I searched for a tragic story: I imagined this woman's daughter had died in a car crash, this was how she'd become so cut off from her humanity.

'Don't you worry,' I whispered. 'I'll find room for his bags.'

'Good,' she said, and I steeled my heart, then smoothed down my skirt.

While I waited for the African man to acknowledge me, a late passenger pushed past knocking me forward. He turned and apologised so profusely, I gave him a smile which made me imagine Mother Theresa.

'Sir,' I said, turning back. 'If I could just move your bags from this side into the lockers above you?'

'Why would we do that?'

'To create room on the right-hand side of the plane. It's a cabin-weight issue.' I felt pleased with myself for concocting something authentic sounding. 12G nodded, waving his hand in the air in an easy-going manner. His children jumped up and down, bumping their seats. 12J and 12K watched as I lugged the bags from one side to the other. The final three took all my strength.

Leaving the spaciousness of business class, I was struck by the packed shoulders of economy. What I'd learnt in training was no longer abstract and happened for real. During the safety demonstration I worried I wouldn't get the double bow right on the life jacket, that the passengers would cotton on to my lack of experience. But when I pointed along the floor of the cabin, flicking fingers at the nearest exits, their faces turned to follow. There were ones who paid no attention. They would be the ones who would die, I figured, which brought a sense of satisfaction.

Without having to ask twice, the passengers showed me their fastened seatbelts, lifting their tops and blankets. To my delight, sat in 40H was a short-haired woman wearing khaki trousers with large-zipped pockets, which was the latest lesbian fashion. I realised she might be the only other gay woman on the plane. Her bag was between her feet on the floor, and I briefly considered letting her get away with keeping it there just in case she might like me. Still she didn't acknowledge me, even though I was stood right over her.

'That'll have to go up I'm afraid,' I said, pointing to her bag. 'You're sat by the emergency exit.'

As if we had all the time in the world, she began rummaging, pulling out a notebook, tissues, then repositioned a set of keys into the inner pocket, all before buckling up the bag. The instructors had said how during an emergency evacuation, passengers would hold onto their personal possessions, hold up the aisle while saving their belongings, believing in the safety of objects.

'You can take it down after take-off,' I said, tucking loose strands of my bob behind my ear, hoping she might notice the giveaway style. Instead she slotted a black gel pen into the spiral of her notebook, wedging it between her legs.

'I do like those pens,' I said.

'Yep, they're good,' she replied.

'The way the ink glides over the page, like you can't stop drawing . . .'

She moved her hand over the items, probably unconsciously, but I regretted my comment. It was wrong here, something I would've said at art college, or on my travels; the words no longer matched the me here.

Cabin crew seats for take-off.

The lights dimmed to low, and the day outside was leaving for tomorrow. As the plane turned onto the runway, the glow from the sunset was cut into shapes by the window frames, and russet-coloured glints moved over the tops of passengers' hair. Looking along the cabin from my seat, rows and rows of people were lit. They were both my audience and my spectacle. It was quite something to me.

The engines roared and the power mounted through my shoes. To the side of the runway, the grass flattened then a flock of birds lifted off. I hoped they wouldn't get sucked into the engines but also did want to know if it would smell of chicken like the trainers said it would.

As the plane gathered speed, I began to count: one, two, three, hoping we would take off when I got to ten. But at fifteen we were still pounding over the ridges in the runway. Twenty-four, twenty-five, my heart raced – surely we would be out of runway soon? Then the plane gently rose, the ground becoming parked planes, fields, and cars snaking along the motorway. Red tail-lights one way, white head-lights the other. Before long, we were over the coast and the specked glow of Brighton pier. I thought of all the gay bars and the women down there. Then the sea was a dark sheet and the white chalk cliffs a slight step lifting out of the dark.

The Spanish stewardess strode up the aisle and the passengers watched as I rose from my seat, the plane at such an angle I had to lean into it to be able to walk.

'If you want to have a fag before we begin, now's your chance.' Peter tapped a packet of Marlboro Red. All five of us from economy huddled behind a curtain. I'd never smoked without alcohol before, and it wasn't good, but I wanted to be part of what they were doing. Peter talked about the karaoke in the hotel bar and the AIDS orphanage, where he was taking supplies, and how not to eat the salad from room service. Nairobi was a good trip, there would be a room party on arrival, so I should get crew-purchase miniatures before disembarkation. At the end of the trip we got a free pineapple and a bag of coffee beans courtesy of the hotel, but I should check for spiders.

The lights came on full and Peter ripped off the cellophane and poured hot water over trays of hot towels. A series of TV monitors dropped from the ceiling. Starting the drinks round, I noticed how the foiled snacks were ripped open and people scattered them over napkins like picnics. Plastic lids were snapped open on the miniatures and I offered double doubles. *Titanic* began to play on the TV monitors, and I gave the gay woman in 40H two packets of nuts with two cans of lager and then a quarter bottle of Champagne 'for whenever'. She seemed to brighten at the Champagne, but she was still a bit distant, probably because she assumed I was straight.

After the meal, I asked passengers to lower their blinds. Night had properly fallen after a prolonged period where we'd flown with the sunset. Peter closed the galley curtains using the press stud, but still people came in wanting socks, newspapers, or to zap some baby milk in our non-existent microwave. During a break in the action, I sat chewing a steak from business class and watched the moonlight bounce off the wing. I wondered if I would feel its effect more, since I was so much closer.

A little while later the back of the plane began to populate itself and passengers collected in the space by the toilets. There was talk of a party, which at first was accepted. Peter said passengers often drank themselves back to their seats and when I passed the crowd, I felt the ease of friendships forming over whiskey and beers, sharing out of cigarettes.

They puffed away as the passengers in front sat in the enveloping fog – but no one complained.

When the film *Titanic* began for a second time, I glanced at the screen to find Kate Winslet posing naked for Leonardo DiCaprio. He was sketching her breasts in pencil, and I remembered when I life modelled at art college, seeing it as a natural step towards my art career. There was that autumn term when the tutor had commented on my body filling out. Though I kept turning up for the work, I hadn't felt comfortable doing it again.

A lot of the passengers were now asleep, and it struck me how odd it was, them with their eyes closed with the Titanic not yet sunk. We were suspended mid-air, watching a disaster movie, and they were all adrift elsewhere.

Soon the party became so loud a passenger complained they couldn't hear the film through their headphones. Peter suggested I take down a tray of water to sober them up. Wandering to the back with sixteen tumblers balanced on the tray, feeling for trip hazards with my toes, I studied the party of mainly men for signs of aggression. With Dad, I'd seen the sudden flare after the one too many. How he would turn and accuse me of things, or suddenly send me to bed. Of course, that was when I was younger, but I still feared him. Soon I would have my own place, this job would grant me that freedom.

Each of the passengers took a glass of water dutifully. I noticed a couple of women had joined the group and was amazed how they respected my authority. Then, as I checked behind the toilet doors for terrorist notes, I overheard a conversation.

'We always fly this airline, because of the service. Going down the pan a bit though.'

'They want you to enjoy it because they all love a drink,' the other noted.

'I once saw a crew pissed up in Barbados. We were in the same hotel. One of them was naked, surfing his suitcase across the pool.'

When I appeared out of the toilet they placed their empty tumblers back on the tray, and waited in silence for me to go, but I wanted to hear the stories. I wanted to be part of the story.

In the end we asked the captain to put on the seatbelt sign to force them back to their seats. After everyone had gone, I stood at the back of the plane, watching the film and the lights go out on the sinking ship. Leonardo DiCaprio froze and began to drift from Kate Winslet. While I passed up the cabin, I heard the chorus of pan pipes playing out collectively through the passenger's headsets and pretended it was the soundtrack to my own life.

During crew rest I lay on the bottom bunk with the navy curtain pulled closed. Something which sounded like the sea rushed past. The wall curved with a gap leading to the darkness within the metal fuselage. I had seen a photo of soldiers on the floor of an aircraft without seats or aisles – no window-dressing – just the metal structure arched as cavernous as a whale's belly. There had been talk on the training course about how a particular aircraft was haunted by a stewardess. I heard a clicking noise so lifted my head, realising how unnatural it was to be awake all night. A series of red lights pulsed on the emergency torches.

However hard I tried, I couldn't find the way into sleep. Head aching from tiredness, I climbed down the vertical ladder to the seated area below. A stewardess was pulling up her tights.

'Can't sleep?' she said.

I shook my head.

'It takes some getting used to – the morgue upstairs. It's arctic tonight.'

She had on matching bra and knickers like a lingerie model. Her breasts were small, and she didn't have pubic hair. As I pulled off my t-shirt revealing black cotton knickers and a non-matching bra, I hunched over in case she saw. I forced myself to stop staring. I wondered why her underwear made me feel so uneasy and put my t-shirt back on until I could get to the coat hanger with my uniform on it.

'I'm Nicky by the way,' she said. 'It's your first flight, isn't it?'

I nodded as she put in her earrings. Pearl studs. No hoops allowed.

'Bet your boyfriend will miss you?'

Through the partition wall came the suck thump whoosh of the toilet flush of the passenger toilet. Someone was taking their usual morning dump.

'Oh, I'm gay,' I said, thinking how I should be able to say it. There were plenty of gay male stewards, surely because of this it was a liberated workplace.

'Right,' she said, thinking. She pulled out a lip gloss and started to dab it on. 'Look, between us, I don't mind, but I wouldn't go spreading that sort of thing about. The girls don't like it.'

'Really?' I said, my stomach dropping as if the plane was suddenly in descent. I didn't apologise, even though I felt I could. She left soon after that. I guessed she thought she was being kind, letting me into the female ways of the airline, but leaning over the small crew sink, I wanted to vomit. A tight band crept round my forehead. I brushed my teeth then smoothed down my bob. I disliked the wisps around my ears, how they made me look fluffy. With a band I fastened the hair into a ponytail, as small as a stubble brush. Expanding a navy scrunchie around my fingers, I studied it, knowing I had to wear it over the band. My bob was too long over my collar to wear down. In the manual it stated plaits or ponytails secured with a single piece of elastic with no protective covering were unacceptable. But why was the ruched material so horrible? Was it the actual word 'scrunchie'? It was a nasty word, implied making yourself smaller, crinkled, contracted.

Unsure whether I was being irrational – it was four in the morning – I couldn't ask anyone what they thought about the significance of hair bands and femininity. The L Gang were out at a club in Soho. When I'd told them about my job they'd been surprised, shocked even, but not said anything much else.

Alone in front of the mirror, I found a button which gave extra light and began to apply lipstick. Peter was writing my assessment. At art college I'd posed as different characters, worn fake moustaches, worn blonde wigs and dark sunglasses, before graduating onto the impersonation of drag queens with false eyelashes. I'd learnt how a face could be put on by the Welsh BBC make up department, convincing audiences into believing I was a female impersonator, a man impersonating a woman. Could this job be part of the same investigation? What it is like for a woman to impersonate another type of woman? And could a job become a form of one's art?

Opening the crew rest door, the light dazzled, so I shaded my eyes with my hand. Passengers were queuing for the toilets all the way along the aisle. A man glanced into crew rest behind me, so I quickly shut the door. I pushed carefully along the cabin, fighting the rising tide of passengers. On the drop-down screens the credits were rolling on *Only Fools and Horses*. I knew I had to be cheerful. In the vain hope of Peter peering through the curtain, I stooped to pick up a stray sock.

'Miss?'

'Yes?' I said, turning. 43B had his hand raised.

'Can I have a glass of water please?'

'Of course,' I said.

Biscuit. Talcum powder. Landing card. The call bells ignited, and the requests kept coming. *Yes, yes*, I said. In the end I carried out a tray of drinks, passing them to those I could remember. Now the cabin was awake and the last of the window blinds pushed up, the day began, regardless of having had no sleep.

'Don't pour any more out,' Peter said, as he switched on the ovens. 'They'll get a juice cuplet with their breakfast. Have a coffee. Get yourself ready, and make sure that curtain stays closed.'

As I yanked it across, I could feel the passenger's anticipation on the other side, waiting for me to reappear. In my mind I heard, *you are not doing enough.*

'I need the loo,' I said.

Peter nodded. 'Use business class. But don't go into First. It's so quiet, even a whisper in the galley can be heard by the passengers.'

'Thanks,' I said, thinking how I didn't want to run into Nicky. Especially if she had told the other stewardesses about me.

I walked to business class and discovered a cubicle with a green vacant sign. It smelt acrid like a men's urinal. After

I sat down, I realised the floor was soaked. When I was finished, I pressed the button under the mirror, swinging it open so my image disappeared to the side. Here was the water shut-off valve, there was the air freshener, so I sprayed the toilet liberally with the citrus freshener and mopped the floor with hand towels under my shoe, wondering whether this might be good to mention to Peter.

In the cabin came the smell of bacon cooking. Peter explained the colour coding on the hot breakfasts, red foil cover for full English, green for the omelette. Pushing my trolley through the curtain, it jolted over the ridge rattling the tea and coffee pots. I could feel the passenger's eyes on me, hunting like animals, but I kept my gaze straight ahead in case they asked for anything. Before leaving the galley Peter had said, 'sell the omelette'. He'd also told me to keep up with the Spanish stewardess on the other side. She didn't talk to anyone more than she had to and lacked a fundamental joy. Everyone would want the English breakfast, he said, but there wasn't enough to go round.

'Good morning sir, mushroom omelette with sauté potatoes . . .?' I lowered my voice, so the next sentence was muffled. 'Or the full English?'

Full English full English full English – it took on the motion of a train. Not one omelette was taken by the time I was twenty passengers in. And I tried not to care, knowing how little this should matter in the scheme of things. Every time I tried to make the potatoes sound delicious by using a part-French accent. 'Sautéed.' But by the time I reached midway, I was fighting a losing battle. Back in the galley, I asked Peter for more, knowing it would go against me.

'Already?' Peter said. 'You're not using the word "mushroom" are you?'

'No, well, yes. Sometimes.'

'That puts people off, at this hour.'

I suddenly felt very upset, more upset than I should've. Peter went unhappily through the shelves seeing what was left.

'Here you go,' he said, dropping a few into my plastic canister. 'I'll need to keep some back for the others.'

I counted twelve disappointed faces who reluctantly took the omelette, but when I reached 47F there was a complete gear change. An elderly man with the air of an army colonel demanded the 'proper breakfast'. His tone bruised the air around him and the woman adjacent tittered, as wives do, to balance out the bad moods. She said how she *loved* omelette. I remembered my training and tried to imagine he was family but could only think of Dad. I felt a sulk come on and had to override it, pretending to be nicer than I felt. In the end I went to Peter and asked him to speak to 47F.

Peter spent a while placating the man. But then, treacherously, he went and brought a meal from first class hidden under blue paper towel. Though the passenger had treated me badly, there was his reward on a china plate: two slices of quality back bacon, fluffy scrambled egg, button mushrooms *and* a hash brown. As I carried it to 47F, I concealed it from the other passengers. Of course 47F merely nodded, then ripped open the salt sachet and poured it over the bacon. Of course this was how the world worked, he shouted so he got what he wanted, while we were all too polite, too paid to take it or do anything about it.

It was at this moment I knew, if I was going to survive this job, I had to toughen up and be more resilient. Be less emotional in order to make everything easier.

Before landing Peter positioned a bottle of sparkling

water next to a carton of apple juice, then handed me a paper cup full of cold liquid. Bubbles popped on my nose before I smelt the Champagne.

'Landing drinks,' he said. 'Be quick.' I drank it hurriedly. Although it slightly hurt, it ignited something vertical, like the idea there could be a brilliant future. As we drank, he showed me all the ticked boxes on my assessment. Ninety-six percent, which he said was the highest score possible, because the company would mistrust him if he gave a hundred.

Coming into land, I pressed my face to the window and took in the palm trees and banks of orange earth. I spotted a flamingo, then a crane flying onto the roof of the airport building. I felt love. I was at last in Africa and so beamed a sincere smile to the tens of passengers as they left. The cleaners came crowding down the aisles in white hairnets and overalls, carrying brushes and buckets of cleaning fluid. I tried to say hello, catch their eye, know their names, but they weren't interested and rushed straight past.

'Darling, could you check the overhead lockers on the left-hand side please?' Peter said, shoving the empty Champagne bottle into a dirty meal trolley. It was the Spanish stewardess' side and therefore her responsibility to check, but she was nowhere to be seen. Still, I opened the overhead bins, running my hand carefully inside in case of syringe needles. When I got to the middle of the aircraft, I opened a door and discovered a pair of shins in navy tights. Opening the adjacent cover, a stewardess appeared curled on her side in a ball.

'Surprise!' she said. It was Nicky. The crew filed out cheering and clapping. She balanced her feet on the seat arms, then sprang to the floor.

'You've not seen anything yet,' she said, touching my shoulder. 'You're lucky we didn't do the shitty nappy.'

Because of the sea of delighted faces, I laughed too, but the ritual hinted at the humiliations found at a boarding school. Still they were being inclusive, but forceful like a presentation of a birthday cake from strangers.

Once in the airport, security waved us through the crew lane without checking our passports. Outside the terminal the earth was sun-baked and the air thick with diesel and humidity. I followed Peter to the waiting minibus.

Soon we were on our way from the airport. The smooth road turned to a bumpy dust track with bony-shouldered cows and roadside shacks selling juice in goldfish bags. At the junction whole rows of marble gravestones were propped up for sale. When the bus overtook a group of locals in the back of a pickup truck, I slid open my window and gripped the ledge, smelling wood smoke.

'Jambo,' one of the men shouted, his teeth full of gaps. I smiled, shyly. Overwhelmed at making contact with an actual local, I quickly shut the window.

As if there was no Africa outside, as if this was so every day it was invisible, the crew passed round plastic cups of Bucks Fizz. I sipped the bitter drink, then tried 'Brown Milk' – a mix of Baileys, brandy, and chilled milk. The first officer unclipped his tie and the driver put on 'Dancing Queen'. One by one, we began to sing until even the captain had joined in. When the song finished, he stood, the bus rocking him from side to side, and announced there was to be a party in his room on arrival.

On reaching the Intercontinental, I was nice drunk but wanted more to stop it from sinking. While we waited in the marbled reception for our room keys, I studied the African jewellery on sale outside the gift shop. There were postcards with the BIG FIVE animals superimposed next to one another. I would send one to Mum, tell her everything: how the hotel sofas were covered in leopard print, how the air smelt of dusty sun-baked roads. I got an urge to convey how life at home with Dad was so small, that there was a whole wide world for her to visit. It felt hard to understand how their lives and this place could exist concurrently.

Finally, the receptionist called me over and handed me a folded paper pouch with my name on it. The CSD came close and said to write down what room she was in, should I need her. Then I noticed Peter queuing for Kenyan Shilling. I guessed he was taking out money on his Diners Card for the trip now, rather than doing it later, but I wanted to see my room.

I took the lift to the second floor and followed the corridor until I found my door. The room was in darkness and smelt of lacquer with a distant residue of cigarettes. The curtains were pulled to keep the room cool from the sun. I found the switch and so many lights came on at once. The bed was covered in a faded green bedspread. It was the third time I'd ever been in a hotel room, and the first which wasn't paid for by Dad.

The bathroom smelt of recent cleaning fluid and I spotted the free shampoo. Then I opened a small cardboard box to find a shower cap. I tried it on for size, then used an ear bud. Two rolled white flannels sat next to two glasses, a set for couples.

I went round the room barefoot, dodging a dark patch on the carpet by the desk. Opening the wardrobe I hummed the song from *Titanic*. The pain from wearing heels was sharp across my feet so I held onto the door to examine the dry-cleaning bag. We could get our inflight gilets cleaned for free if we hung them outside our door in time. I wrote out the slip, nervous part of my uniform might get lost.

Pulling back the curtains to the Kenyan sun, I slid open the door to a find a narrow balcony, deep enough for half my feet. The sunlight hit my tights, so I pulled them off, leaving them in a ball. I could keep them on the floor for three full days if I wished. The room overlooked the hotel car park and beyond were pavements peopled with locals heading to work. To my amazement, there was a park with a grass lawn, and cedar trees. People wandered in such brazen sunshine. Light took eight minutes to travel all the way from the sun – you could believe that in London – but here it seemed faster, more immediate. The locals were probably thinking about what they would have for lunch, the everyday people of Kenya, and I realised how I could never have imagined any of this. The simultaneous movements of the world needed to be experienced first-hand. Millions of people walking around in different places at every point of the day was mind-blowing. I would never be able to convey all this on a postcard.

When I slid the door shut, the air conditioning was liberating. I became busy clipping my uniform to the non-detachable coat hangers when there was a knock at the door. The bellboy wheeled in my suitcase, lifting it onto a rack, which felt intimate, him here in my room, so I stood blocking the view of my tights on the floor. He hesitated and I knew to tip him one US dollar, so I found my purse and pulled out a green note. For a moment we held it between us. He then nodded, wordless. When he left I listened to him knock on the adjacent doors, repeating the same delivery of airline cases, and I realised I was surrounded by my crew.

I wasn't sure what to do first, so I took a shower, then came out of the bathroom, wrapped in a towel, hanging one round my neck like a boxer post-fight. The mini bar had a fake wooden door. Inside was empty and only slightly cool to the touch. On top were two upturned glasses on paper coasters. From my wheelie suitcase I pulled out the duty free bag filled with eighteen miniatures and mixer cans. I poured out vodka, filling it up with Diet Coke. It was not yet nine a.m., but I had to reconnect with the bus alcohol. Sitting on the mattress, I could've said out loud, *this is the life*, but they were not my words. Immediately I stood up, the bed too tempting.

Through the miracle of drink, I felt really healthy, so I dressed quickly then left for the room party. Running my hand over the wall of the corridor, I studied the print in the carpet, noting how the runner finished and the polished wooden floor showed either side.

By the lift was a wooden sculpture of a long-faced tribesman. Cynically, I expected it to be stuck to the table, but it came up in my hand. This was a hotel which trusted its guests not to steal the ornaments. 'Hello,' I said in my mind to the sculpture. Then I sniffed his face and found my tongue darting out to taste the varnish. When the lift pinged, I put him back down, after drying him against my top.

Once in the elevator, I pressed the button for the top floor. Noticing in the mirror a kink in the back of my hair, I tried to comb it out with my fingers. Surely no one would wash and redo their hair for the room party? I turned from the mirror – I didn't want to know what I looked like to others. Something like a sudden shadow took hold, so I patted my back pocket to check for the room key. There it was, the plastic warming. Safe.

Still, I couldn't turn back to my mirror image. So when the lift arrived and the doors parted, I hopped over the ledge, racing from it as quickly as I could.

CHAPTER 3

The Pretend Christmas

LGW – MEX – LGW

At 40,000ft above sea level, I found myself balancing thirty dirty plastic coffee cups on a tray, dreaming of how, when my life was recorded in an artist's compendium, it would count as the longest piece of durational performance art in the history of the 20th Century. I could be a working-class version of the artist Tehching Hsieh, who for a whole year in his studio in 1980, punched a clock on the hour, every hour. I had read about it as part of my degree, how it could be described as 'waiting art' – work that addressed what it meant to live with uncertainty and keep going, often with no clear end in sight.

The aircraft began its descent, and I got the budding sensation I always got – something like nearing a tiny conclusion. I pressed my forehead against the window and noticed three mouse-shaped clouds over the tawny mountain range below. We weren't far off Mexico City, and this was the trip I had been waiting for. Mexico wasn't just any destination: it offered mysticism, Frida Kahlo, Aztec ruins, spontaneous fiestas, women trekking naked in the mountains (I had seen a TV documentary), and an inkling – confirmed years later – that Patricia Highsmith had lived around here.

Earlier, over the wide expanse of the North Atlantic Ocean, a passenger had pressed his call bell three times in quick succession. When I'd arrived at his seat, it was not the heart attack I half-expected (would I ever get to use the defibrillator?) but the passenger appeared agitated, pointing his finger down at the sea. He asked a question in Spanish, and when I shook my head the woman next to him translated.

'Why isn't the plane moving?' she asked on his behalf.

'I can guarantee we are moving,' I said, while the woman carried on interpreting. 'You would certainly know if we were not.' And then this odd chuckle came out my mouth, and I thought, *that's new.*

The woman chatted on in Spanish as the man nodded. Still I took his point. While cruising, out of the window there was a luminous white banner of horizon and we could sometimes observe the plane's shadow on the tops of clouds, but with no houses or trees speeding by, being in motion was difficult to grasp.

This encounter summed up what was happening to me more and more frequently: passengers asked me questions, which in turn made me ask bigger ones, ones with more than one answer or no answer at all. I'd begun to realise how easily time got mislaid, so I'd started writing things down on hotel notepads. Sometimes they were observations, like how senior crew rarely glanced out of the windows and would only look out of the aircraft for Mount Kilimanjaro or the Northern Lights. But often when I read back through my notes, they were drunken hieroglyphics, passionate thoughts lost in the moment.

Steve, my steward friend for this flight, was a glass-half-full kind of person. Even though he struck me as familiar, of course I'd never met him before. In the briefing room, I'd spied him immediately as a gay man. And he was stunning, like an actor who would be perpetually cast in Hollywood to play the tennis coach. He had a history of flying, starting with a budget airline, then leaving for the better pay of our premium airline. I was envious at how he spoke about the ladder of his career so proudly, with no sarcasm or embarrassment.

Across the Tannoy, the landing announcement began first in English, then in Spanish. I made out 'Por favor' as I walked backwards, checking seatbelts, motioning my finger for seatbacks to come forward. Nowadays, I was in harmony with the service, and did the job effortlessly.

We had a quick landing drink in the galley and Steve joked about the man in 47C who had asked him to rinse his trousers in the onboard washing machine. Some people believed we had a fully formed kitchen and did the washing up as we went along. A lot of people believed we were nannies and cleaners, but I didn't record these kind of details in my notebook because they were too zapping.

The cabin was silent, with that distinct holy quiet which descent brought. Steve was strapped in by doors five left and the sunlight streamed in across his white shirt. My crew seat faced the tail of the plane and the passengers in E zone. With the click-shut of my harness, I checked round the emergency exit. Then Steve gave me a little wave, and I lifted my chin with a grin. Again the butterflies, the high of a potential friend. Earlier, when the crew had gone on first break, Steve and I had eaten side-by-side, creamy chicken korma with naan bread. He'd begun to tell me about his partner, Rob. (Crew used the word 'partner' as code for gay relationships.)

'Rob also once flew for a living. We met at Airtours and had the best time. Holidays in Thailand and Florida. We were often away when we could fit in a quick break, but then he goes off sick and gets this dog. Then he develops an odd burping. Reflux. And now he doesn't leave the dog. He'll go for a walk, as far as the pier. Stays there for hours, watching. We used to have fun. But anyway, enough of the jump seat therapy. You got a boyfriend?'

My stomach contorted. Every flight, at least once a week, the script came at me about a boyfriend. Sure, the question held less pressure from a gay man, but still it was a constant stress.

'Jump seat therapy?' I asked, not having heard this expression before.

'Yeah. When we tell each other all sorts, fast. You know things people would usually take months to tell their friends, we say it all in the first hour. So, anyone at home?'

'Not at the moment.' The only story I could think of was the recent one-night stand with a woman who had ended up with a slipped disc. I had told her I knew innately how to give massages, which at the time I'd believed was true.

'Oh. You're not?'

'What?'

'Flat shoes.' He gestured at my loafers and grinned, nodding. 'Lesbian loafers.'

'No they're not.'

I'd heard this prejudice before. Trousers were now part of the new uniform, yet any woman who chose to wear them with flat shoes was positioned as unglamourous and regarded as lower in all senses than heeled women. Nevertheless, I was as tall as a man and so when I wore heels, I bumped my head on the overhead lockers.

'I'll find you someone this trip,' he said, squeezing my knee. 'My gaydar is very in tune with my surroundings. You're lovely looking. Besides, you know the difference between a straight and a gay?'

'No?'

'About three drinks.'

I groaned, having heard this joke before, but still it had been the most welcoming interaction I'd had since joining. Nicky's comments, although a while back, had left a scar which had affected my behaviour. Steve glowed bright with confidence, he was in his element and free to be himself and I wanted to be like this. His ease reminded me of Mum, but with more open expression. There was a generosity to his mood, and like with Mum, a surface level which meant I couldn't go too deep. There was nothing hidden, I liked the fact he had no sides to him.

As the plane banked, the window became sky. I would never get sick of this rocketeer's viewpoint. Maybe this was the greatest invention – to fly – to imitate a bird and have people pay to sit inside it, like being in its ribcage. The Mexican earth pitched closer, and we flew over a pea-green reservoir, then something dark like a cemetery. As usual, my right breast itched with the shift in cabin pressure. Babies especially felt it in their ears and cried out to let us know. Pretending to brush my nose, I rubbed the area with my wrist. Then I saw the trees quite clearly, and the trucks along the motorway developed distinct windows. A river declared its banks. There were parked aircraft, the red roof of a hut, and finally the edge of the runway.

It was the easiest of landings. The wing flaps went up and I felt the drag as my shoulder straps locked. We rumbled along while cheers broke from a class of students near the back, as if the curtains had swept together on a brilliant show. I loved their unbridled enthusiasm. It made me realise how checked we were in the UK.

Welcome to Mexico City where the local time is . . .alcohol. Earlier in the galley Steve mentioned a tequila bar with fifty distinct types, most so pure they didn't give you a hangover.

The captain had the final word and thanked everyone for flying with us. He was organising a day trip out of Mexico City to a cactus farm, which produced drink from fermented cacti originally for monks. There was a donkey on site, which drank beer all day long. You could buy a *cerveza*, place it on the ground and the donkey would lift it in its teeth, then throw it back. He had laughed at this, as if it weren't cruel, but I knew from Tammy Dog how animals could get addicted to lager. Dad would take her out, give her froth off his fingers. We had to let the captain know if we wanted to go. I didn't like the idea of sombreros at lunch. Mexicans probably thought holidaymakers who did this were stupid, and I was determined never to become a tourist.

As we taxied towards the gate, a man in 40C got up while the plane was still moving so, I told him to take his seat. He started whistling 'California Dreaming', and by the time he was buckled back in, the seat belt sign had gone off. This made me feel petty, as if I'd made up the rule, rules

55

I wasn't even sure I wanted to implement half the time. Seemingly not irritated, he retrieved a cowboy hat from the overhead bin.

While we waited to disembark, I could tell the passenger was meditating on my hat. I'd pressed myself into the space by the door, trying to keep all eyes off me. Exhausted, I didn't want to be the television they gawped at anymore. I'd read somewhere once as hunter-gatherers we would never have met more than two hundred people in our lives, that there was a natural limit to what was right to our social interactions. There were so many dizzying moments like this one, me jostled alongside the passengers, trying to find room away from the intensity of so many lives being lived in any one moment.

Breathing in any remaining patience, I remembered to be aware of the effect I was giving out. The company had drilled into us how disembarkation was the most vital moment of the flight. How we acted during this final stage formed lasting memories and could erase anything negative the passenger may have experienced. As a final goodbye, our smiles should be natural and available, freely beamed on regardless of how we felt. I had practiced in the mirror, trying to see if I could spot insincerity in the corners of my mouth. So far, I'd been unable to fake warmth in my reflection. There was still time.

'Have you been to Mexico City before?' I said to 40C. Soon there would be drinks on the bus. I let calm seep into my face.

'Yes, I live here. Much better life than in the States. I'm a migrant, in reverse. You?'

I shook my head.

'Make sure you stop off at Casa Azul in San Angel. Boy,

the garden has magical qualities. It was Frida Kahlo's place. Fuchsia, sunflowers, all alongside lime trees. There's a fence of cacti erected around the house. Healed my sister's broken heart, her sitting alongside the Jacarandas. You'll know what I mean when you see it. Here.'

From out of his pocket he handed me a battered business card. Printed on it was his name, Jo Space, his phone number and then simply, ARTIST. I nodded then slipped the card in my inner jacket pocket, wondering what kind of art he made. I was sure no one bona fide handed out cards calling themselves an artist, in the way you would call yourself a plumber or an estate agent. Rather ungenerously, I imagined oil paintings of sunset horses dashing along beaches. But he did know about Frida Kahlo, and not many people seemed to take her seriously.

'Thank you,' I said, quickly, feeling prickled by jealousy. Surely, I could say I was an artist on a business card? I could be that person. There was an element of forging your own way in the world I had not realised until then. On my last flight I had met the man with the longest moustache in the world. Like heavily overweight people, he'd had to book an extra seat for extra width. I had taken a blurry photo on my mobile phone of the waxed hair protruding from either side of his face. Using wire, he said, was seen as cheating. He was in the Guinness Book of Records and said he travelled the world being invited to show it off.

On the coach from the airport I showed Steve the business card, expecting him to take the rise out of it because so many people seemed to dismiss art as nothing other than airy fairy nonsense. We were alongside one another sipping 'bus juice', our tiredness getting obliterated by the alcohol. I told him what the man had said about Frida Kahlo's house, how I knew she painted wombs and flowers. How I wanted to go.

'I don't know why he gave the card to me,' I said, hoping for a compliment.

Steve said, 'Of course he gave it to you, because you're beautiful. He probably wanted to have sex with you.' I didn't blush like some heterosexual girls might, even though this transaction felt like it belonged to a straight girl and boy.

The coach drove down wide avenues and past narrow streets, and I wondered what was my fascination with Steve? When I rested my elbow against his, I hoped he felt the electricity, how aware we both were of the skin under our shirt sleeves. We were both gay, so nothing could ever happen, but I hadn't felt this level of wanting someone to take an interest for such a long time. It was like the sun finding your face after a long grey winter.

The Sheraton Maria Isobel was over an hour away. It was fortunate that flights dehydrated us, since there was never a toilet stop and yet so much liquid consumed. Eventually we arrived at a roundabout and stepping down from the coach I found the Angel of Independence gazing down, her polished golden wings outspread. A hot queue of cars and taxis pushed on by. Outside the hotel, a man played on a drum kit with cymbals and a mouth organ all attached to his body. It moved as he did.

Because of multiple trips to Houston and Dallas, I knew the Sheraton colour scheme and how this chain of hotels positioned their shower curtains, so they never clung to your legs. They also provided enough face flannels to secrete one home. Mum was building a good collection for the odd nights family came to stay.

Tradition demanded a room party. Today's host was our young on-board manager, Maggie, a DJ in her spare time who lived in Brighton. Soon we were sat on her room floor, drinking crew purchase, flicking cigarette ash into empty soda cans. I was near the curtains with four gay male crew and when I could, I slipped it into the conversation that I was gay. Even though their response was warm, I kept an eye out for Steve. When he finally arrived, he entered wearing roller blades, opening his arms past the TV cabinet, singing 'Starlight Express'. As he bent down to unfasten the laces, he tripped and landed sideways on the bed. The crew were in uproar, and I helped him up, loosening his laces, feeling possessive when I touched them. Steve explained how he brought the skates on most trips to exercise. He thought the skating might help his balance. It was then I got the idea to go back to my room to do a little show myself. Here I put on the drag eyeshadow, contoured my cheeks, then pulled a sheet off my bed, tying it around me in a knot. I unscrewed the lampshade from the standard corner lamp, and went back to the party where I made an entrance from the corridor, performing a haphazard lip sync to Shirley Bassey's 'I Am What I Am'. After, I told them I had once impersonated women at art college, which was at first seen by the crew as out there, but soon became something I was renowned for down route.

All of this happened before six p.m.

It wasn't long before we had run out of drink, so we headed back to our rooms to get ready to go out. Our gang of gay crew met in the foyer. We'd hatched a separate plan from the rest of the crew, especially out of the captain's earshot. As we waited to draw out Pesos from reception, a mariachi band played to business travellers in the bar. The noise was intense. Even so, I liked the violins, trumpets, and fast guitars and how the energetic old men were dressed in black bolero jackets and matching trousers with white trim. The lead singer was a woman in her sixties in traditional Mexican floor-length dress, clapping her hands fast, her hair pulled back slickly with a single rose clipped at the side. As we passed by, I caught her eye and she applauded her hands towards me, making me do a little run. Steve watched this, beaming; he seemed to notice everything about me.

Opposite the hotel was a street the crew knew well. Seedy and dark, a bar called 'Lips' was halfway down, but when we got there it was closed. We hailed a yellow Beetle taxi and piled in, all five of us, the smallest spread across our laps as we headed merrily to the Zocalo.

Swinging from side to side a rosary hung from the taxi driver's rear-view mirror. There was no call for seat belts as the cab crawled through the busy streets, passing what seemed to be the entire population of the city. Soon we began to sing 'La Bamba', ensuring the alcohol feeling didn't drift, and the taxi driver tapped his steering wheel in an easy manner.

We were eventually dropped at the edge of the main square, and we stood in awe of the crowds. On the right was a party, or was it a protest? Demonstrators waved flags as tinny music played from radios. It didn't feel dangerous, just more alive, and more expressive than England. But this wasn't what we were after, so we found a stall selling rum mixed with fruit juice. Steve bought two cups and the man stuck straws in the tops with a squeak.

'Come on,' Steve said, handing me one.

'Where to?' I said, sipping it. Lime, ice, sugar, mint. Yes, there was lots of good alcohol.

'Follow me,' he said, grabbing my arm. He was an inch taller than me, and I liked the sense of security his height gave me.

'Shouldn't we wait for the others?'

'They'll find us.'

We barged through the crowd passing people banging pots with spoons. One person jumped on a box and yelled something into a loudspeaker. It hurt my ears, so I motioned to Steve for us to head near some tourists outside the National Palace. From their bum bags, Bermuda shorts and white trainer socks, the group were clearly American.

'Diego Rivera was asking all Mexicans to look squarely at the history of their lives, he understood the beauty in the struggle, and misery and pain . . .' The tour guide explained, competing with the racket.

When I turned, the other crew were nowhere to be seen. I was pleased because I wanted nothing more than to drink and hold Steve's arm. My understanding of my sexuality was so limited, I hadn't figured in a hybrid variety. At the same time, I knew these feelings weren't allowed to be explored. The L Gang at home would have it I should be a hundred percent lesbian, but the jumping sensation in my stomach proved otherwise. And here it was again when he turned to check I was okay, an undeniable flood of warmth. Sanguine. Didn't the word come from sangria? Blood? Life.

When we finished our drinks Steve mentioned the Zona Rosa, so we headed to a bar called '*El Amacen*', which he had written on a piece of paper. At the door, we paid the cover charge and went into a room dark with wood panelling. It took a moment for our eyes to adjust to the soft amber lighting. After getting a drink we stood by the jukebox, which turned out to be broken but created a light source.

As usual it was only men, and so I suggested we go down-stairs in search of women. But the basement contained only more men, who eyed Steve as we passed, the short corridor leading towards a closed door.

'Dark room,' Steve said, his eyes brightening.

'Photographic?' I said, with my eyes widening playfully.

'No cameras allowed, I expect,' he said.

'I want to see inside,' I said, realising he hadn't got my joke. We began queuing behind men who didn't appear particularly gay but looked like most of the Mexicans I'd seen in the street. When we got to the front, since I was female, I wasn't let in. I shooed Steve to go ahead, saying I would wait upstairs. As I left him, I hoped he'd insist on coming with me, but he didn't and of course, he shouldn't want to. So I took the stairs, chastising myself for even thinking all of this.

Upstairs a large cluster of drunk Mexican women sailed in loudly as if an uprising were taking place. I waited, trying to make out if there was anyone half-decent, but they were all short and speaking so fast they didn't even notice me. I had my hair in bunches and knew my lipstick gave off the wrong impression. Plus there was my height, a tall cactus towering over land shrubs. No one gave me a second look, so I leant on the jukebox, inspecting the songs typed on bits of card. At least twelve had '*amor*' in the title.

Steve wasn't long and I quite enjoyed my time alone. When he pushed through the crowd, he had a grave look on his face. Over the noise he shouted he'd had his wallet stolen and we should head back to the hotel.

In the taxi he was very quiet, watching the world pass by the window. I imagined the men moving their hands over his back and legs, over his jean pockets; how electrifying it must've been, even though they were looking to steal. Even in the dark they would have seen him coming with his blonde hair and Abercrombie & Fitch t-shirt which smelt of washing powder. I shifted closer, angry because the men had shortened our evening and time together. Plus they had access to a sexual experience I couldn't have with Steve. I checked my purse, pulling out notes, counting them, hoping it would cover the taxi ride. Did I really want to have sex with Steve, or was I conditioned to understand these feelings only in terms of heterosexual desire? The traffic slowed, and I wondered if everyone spent their lives in transit in Mexico City while the meter ticked on.

Back at the hotel, the receptionist said with regret that theft was a common experience in Mexico City. Then she asked whether we were brother and sister, which made me observe Steve in yet another dimension. We went up to his room, ordered some ice and drank a couple of miniatures. He told me how often these disastrous situations happened to him, and he believed they would continue until he got his aura cleansed. Then to lift the atmosphere, we took it in turns to make the memory of the evening good. I rationalised how the money lost only equalled forty pounds and Steve then said the evening had been top apart from that. But still when I asked, Steve wouldn't give me more details about the dark room and instead got out his printed roster and showed me where he was going next. We decided we would request a trip to Arizona. He said healing by crystals happened in a spiritual mecca called Sedona. At the mention of all this future I became very tired. It was the idea he was going to be elsewhere soon, and his life would be where I couldn't be, and we'd have to wait months for the trip request to come through. He had appeared like a gift. Precariously, and in transit. When I kissed his cheek goodnight, I tried not to feel morose. He held me close, and I could smell his perfumed neck, how in the space from his shoulder to chin there was a whole burrow of warmth.

Leaving Steve's room, the click of his door followed me behind. I walked along running my hand over the wallpaper, wishing I could stretch time. A lone drink might help make the night longer. Tomorrow was our only clear day before heading home the following evening. I hadn't connected with anyone since joining the airline, and now how could I assure it would become long-lasting?

When I reached the rubber plant by the lift, I weighed up whether it was real or fake. The rule I gave myself was that I wasn't allowed to touch the plant, or its earth, until I decided. If the plant turned out to be fake, Steve and I would become the best of friends. I pulled at a leaf, then bent it half. It wouldn't snap, so had to be plastic. Still it was very convincing and the imitation earth in the pot even had a crumbled appearance. But I'd won. And so it was decided. Steve and I were to be set on a mutual flight path together. I found my hotel key card and before slotting it in, glanced along the corridor in the direction of Steve's room. I pictured him cleaning his teeth in front of his bathroom mirror, moving a few strands of his hair aside, thinking about me amongst all this hotel silence.

The next morning we met early in the foyer. We decided not to spend thirty dollars on the hotel breakfast buffet when there were cheaper and more interesting places nearby.

Through the city fumes, the sun shone hot. On every corner someone was selling something. Colourful jumbles of chewing gum, key chains, and sets of steak knives. A couple of blocks from the smart hotel the buildings were crumbling, and the dark arches were filled with men and sideways glances. Workers stood in the street eating corn cake, sipping glasses of porridge. I knew to keep my money divided between my pockets and socks. Soon we found a cantina with fluorescent lighting and canary painted walls. A couple of men were already drinking beer at the bar and the tables were filled with students. We were served fresh mango juice and I ordered *huevos rancheros* – eggs in tomatoes. A basket arrived holding warm tortillas, then a plate of chopped steak and fried potatoes which we hadn't ordered. We copied the students as they mopped their plates with tortilla, piling green chilli salsa on top.

Above Steve's head were two beer bottles mounted on the wall. One was dressed in a miniature wedding dress, the other in a tux. My eye kept going back to the tight frilly lace around the neck of the female bottle, thinking about suffocation and the missionary-style sex I'd once had with a boy on a golf course near Bromley.

'You alright?' Steve asked, and I nodded.

Then, patting my hand, he said with the softest of manners, 'This is on me.' It was this gentleness which made me well up, emphasising how little generosity there had been and for so long.

Instead of going back to the hotel, we decided to do our own thing and seek out Frida Kahlo's house. From the tourist information centre, we took the bus to San Angel, which I'd read had once been separated from the city by water. The bus stopped and started every few minutes or so to let more people on, and it took over an hour to leave the centre. Waves of worry came over me about whether we were making a mistake to go so far from the hotel without telling anyone. Crew usually stuck together for a reason, and the captain was supposed to be asked if we wished to spend an evening away from the hotel. When the wide busy streets turned into leafy boulevards, more European than anything, I became more at ease. When I asked the woman standing beside me for Altavista Avenue, she circled her finger in the air and said, 'El siguiente'. A few moments later, she tapped me on the shoulder and motioned towards the exit.

Altavista Avenue met Palmas Street and we walked until we found a row of high pencil cacti which formed a fence. Behind were the coloured walls of a modernist house, saturated in blues and reds. I made Steve wait as I took out my camera. The sun beat down making him squint until he found his sunglasses. I zoomed out, trying to get the succulents in shot with the edge of the building and the deep blue of the sky. I took four or five different angles, just so I could stay there with the cacti and him in the centre of the frame.

Beyond the courtyard of orange and lime trees was a queue of Mexican school children, but no foreign visitors. I felt proud we were able to assimilate along with the locals without a mariachi band striking up. As we waited to be ushered in, I noticed a small house connected to a larger building via a bridge running between them. The bigger of the two looked new; it was disappointing not to see the original. Once inside it smelt of gloss paint. The black and white photographs on the wall showed a recent renovation. We went around the smaller house first, discovering Kahlo's living quarters. A mirror was tilted over a tiny bed, probably so she could paint her portrait while lying down because of her disabilities from her injuries. In the blue-walled kitchen with daffodil-hued flooring, large clay pots waited on the stove. Oversized wooden spoons tried to suggest the kitchen had only just been recently abandoned; someone had hung tiny ceramic cups on the wall with Frida and Diego painted on them. Two painted doves holding a ribbon hovered above a window. All the information was in Spanish, so it was up to us to interpret what it meant. I felt frustrated by the tidiness, as if we were supposed to believe they had just slipped out, leaving a jug of milk on the side. It stood in contrast to Tracey Emin's bed and how she'd shown the true mess of life. My eye searched behind cupboards for smears, but there was nothing. Steve followed closely behind, each time studying what I'd just run my eye over, as if he wasn't sure how to look. I took my time over the toothbrush holder and small bar of soap, imagining Kahlo's hands touching them.

A bridge joined Kahlo's and Diego Riviera's living quarters. From this I presumed they lived separately then met on the crossing. This seemed like the perfect arrangement for a marriage. Compared to the open plan studio next door, with Riviera's stacks of brushes and huge mocked up murals-in-progress, I wondered if Kahlo's tiny studio had dictated the dimensions of her work. Diego painted vast murals, while Frida painted small rectangular drawings of her insides, with monkeys and cats perched on her shoulder, dense thickets of leaves sprouting from her spine.

When we'd seen enough of Diego's studio, Steve and I wandered around the garden noticing the bougainvillea and mysterious shoulder-height pyramids. Behind these was a thin alley, and I side-stepped along it, hoping to find a forgotten artifact belonging to Frida, like a ceramic pipe. When I came out Steve seemed to be searching for something too, and I began to fantasise we would live together with a bridge between our houses. We were the same age – late-twenties, and both born under a Piscean moon, though I had no idea what kind of music he was into or whether he had hobbies we could share apart from drinking.

We left Casa Azul without postcards, as there was no gift shop. Maybe Mexicans were not as consumerist as other nations. This cheered me, and I felt lighter because of it. Then a topless Mexican drove by in a rattling car and honked his horn loudly, before driving off. Steve and I linked arms, as this reminded us how out of place we must look. Then I felt a bit shaken and wondered whether I needed water, or whether it was because the city was so high above sea level.

Behind a church, in a garden full of flowers, we drank Colas on a stone bench. A gardener tended the plants, cutting the roses with sharp snips. Catholics were entering the church for mass. I decided then, this would be our garden, and each time I came to Mexico I would come and find it.

After the church, our clarity focused by sugar, we found a cantina. Cigarette stubs covered the floor. There were art students and ponytailed hippies with nose rings. A couple sat in the corner with no one watching or minding that they couldn't stop kissing. The server brought over beer without us asking, followed by plates of chillies stuffed with cheese. Then another beer arrived with tortillas and thinly sliced pork in a bittersweet sauce. Before we could ask for 'la cuenta', more beers plus a tequila shot arrived.

The bill came to hardly anything. It was in the heat of the afternoon, and we wound back towards Centro on a bus. I wanted to see Diego Rivera's mural at the Grand Palace, but when we arrived there was another demonstration. It was in the square I saw two British-looking lesbian travellers posing for a photograph. This was as thrilling as spotting two rare birds. Over their shoulders they wore matching backpacks, identical white vest tops and army shorts. Both had lovely wide bottoms. I said to Steve to watch, and I jumped behind them and into their holiday picture. In a few weeks' time, when their film was developed, they would find me, craning my neck, waving, an unknown gay woman joining them for a split second. It heartened me to know my image would be there, hidden in an envelope, waiting to be collected from a photo lab.

'You're funny,' Steve said, and I grinned and pulled him close. He was a kind-hearted soft man, and I hadn't had many of them in my life.

The following day we spent sleeping off a late night. Six hours before call I woke to the light on the hotel telephone flashing. This often meant a delayed call time for pick up, but it turned out Steve had left a voicemail to say he'd done something to his back. I rang to say he should ring Maggie, the on-board manager. She arranged for a medic to come to the hotel and the doctor said Steve had pulled something, possibly stemming from a fall at some point on his roller blades.

Before leaving my room, hair smoothed and face on, I went to help him get dressed. He took an age to answer the door and then when he did, he limped back to the chair. As I knelt down, pulling his trousers up over his knees, then stretching socks onto each feet, I was stunned by the long hairs on his big toes. It struck me how unfemale he really was. Maybe I had been pretending he was a kind of woman so I could accept my intense feelings for him. Pushing on his shoes, I studied his face up close. His forehead was etched in pain, while his mouth tried not to give it away. Ambushed by love, I dipped my head, confused by the emotion. Then I tied his laces, pressing the side of his shoes quickly like a shop assistant, before brushing my uniform trousers clean.

Because Steve was a passenger on the flight home and business class was nearly empty, one of their crew stepped into his position to work in economy. She was a moody woman who was needlessly sharp with the passengers, which only highlighted the lack of Steve. When I got a moment, I popped to see him in the business class cabin. He'd been given strong pain killers for the flight and was sleeping each time I went by. I tucked Scottish shortbread onto his seat tray table, and then, when we were close to landing, I passed him a note with my name and phone number on it. I had met plenty of crew who I'd got on with, each trip forming a little family. At the end of a trip we'd said things like, 'Let's stay in touch.' Meaning it at the time, but the way the job went meant it never really happened. Saying goodbye for me was becoming a problem – it had begun to feel too painful.

With Steve it was different. On our days off we met up when we could. Sometimes we went to a gay pub in Norwood, but I preferred to visit him in Brighton. There was never enough time, but Steve and I understood this and were respectful of not pressurising or guilt-tripping one another. With Christmas in mind, we requested a seven-day trip to Caracas so we could fly to an archipelago of islands called Los Roques. With its white golden sand banks and bright blue waters, we might snorkel round a pink mass reported to be made purely of discarded conch shells. With him as my mooring at the airline, I believed this was as close to happiness as I'd get to for the time being.

Early December was warm, as if the season refused to don its usual outfit. I'd invited Steve to number forty-seven as my plus one for the pretend Christmas dinner and told him not to mention global warming as Dad insisted it was made up. Mum wanted to meet him, and I'd made sure I'd told Dad many funny anecdotes about Steve to offset any potential homophobia.

There had been a big turn of events. I'd just moved into my own flat, made possible because of the secure wage from the airline. No woman in my family had ever afforded to live alone before. The first guest to stay had, of course, been Steve. Mum had passed on an already second-hand brown corduroy sofa bed which folded out into a spongey mattress. Each trip away I bought something for my flat. Like a new lover, I offered it gifts: eggcups from Pottery Barn, dinner plates from Target, an antique soda bottle from Buenos Aires, a fold-out stool from Africa. Mum had finally got her thigh-high giraffe for the hearth.

The morning of the pretend Christmas Steve parked his car at mine, then we walked the short distance to number forty-seven. As I unlocked the front door, the steam from the roasting meat hit our chests.

'Mum?'

'In the kitchen!'

Just like usual Christmas, Dad was round the social club drinking while Mum prepared the meal. It shouldn't have annoyed me, but the way the routine was so immoveable meant it did. From her ears hung a pair of gold, bell-shaped earrings with red ribbon bows, and her hair was blow-dried. It was now completely white, and she wore large bifocal glasses. There was no Tammy Dog running to greet us, so I put Steve's jacket in the cupboard under the stairs, sensing the still of the house. The net was pressed wet against the kitchen window, as Mum disliked it being open while cooking. Walking towards her I judged whether we would embrace. She turned, saying hello, while straining her neck to see Steve.

Wiping her hands on her apron she said, 'Call me Joan.'

'Joan, nice to meet you,' Steve said, leaning towards her, introducing aftershave into their equation. When he hugged her, curiously, she let it happen with gusto.

'Shall I take off my shoes?' he asked. And we looked down at his brown leather lace ups, and I shook my head as if to say, this house is not like that.

'It doesn't matter,' I said.

'I will anyway.' And he went to the front door and returned in soft black socks. He wore a khaki fitted shirt and dark denim jeans. Out of a Tesco carrier bag, he pulled a bunch of yellow roses and a box of After Eight mints.

'You must have told him,' Mum said, peering into the flowers.

'Told him?'

'I had yellow roses on my wedding day.' She breathed in their scent, then placed them alongside the meat carving tray, while looking for a vase.

'Oh, I didn't know that. I wasn't there, remember,' I said, trying to make a joke, but I could see by Steve's face it had fallen flat.

'Well, Steve. I feel you might be a little psychic.'

'Oh?' Steve said. 'Why do you say that?'

'You're the only man to have ever bought me yellow

roses, apart from Jeff. But,' she said, a thought moving round her. 'In fact it would've been my father who paid for my wedding flowers. Not Jeff.' And we stood there while Mum mentally ticked through who, if anyone apart from Grandad, had ever bought her the flowers she liked.

All the time I checked back on Steve, to see how he was responding. We went into the lounge, carrying mugs of tea, waiting for Dad so we could start on the alcohol. When he arrived, he brought in cigarette smoke on his V-necked jumper, which he soon struggled off, messing his hair and lifting the shirt underneath to reveal a belly button as deep as a thumb mark in clay. The waistline of his beige trousers rested under his stomach, and I decided to kiss him, which always felt uncomfortable. But I so wanted to be his daughter again, like I had been so effortlessly when I was little. At any time we could start anew.

From his face I felt stubble against my cheek and wondered why he hadn't shaved, and whether it was a small rebuttal on his part. Although I tried not to, I sniffed for booze and of course it was on his breath, not too strong, but enough to conjure the usual twinning of repulsion and sense of inevitability.

'This is Steve,' I said, motioning.

'Jeff. How do you do?'

They shook hands, like men do, silently.

Steve lifted a duty free carrier bag from the floor. 'I brought you something from South Africa. To say thanks.' He handed Dad the gift, and Dad pulled out a rectangular cardboard box, then slid out the bottle.

'Ten-year-old Port. Well, what about that Joan.'

Mum was not in the room.

'They make it in Johannesburg,' I explained. 'The best.'

'Is that so,' Dad said, and I wanted him to say thank you, but he didn't. He left the customary gap Mum would usually fill.

We moved into the dining room, more cramped than I remembered. Just a glance at the bureau gave me the itch to drink. On the table were the heavy silver knives from the wedding cutlery box. Christmas crackers were angled over each plate and serving mats ran up the centre of the tablecloth.

Dad placed the Port on the sideboard, twisting it round so the label faced front.

'Drink? Steve? Lager?' Dad pulled open the door to the bureau, which was now a scant ghost of the plentiful bar from my childhood. He slid forward four cans of super strength German pilsner. Apart from the cans and a bottle of Martini Rosso, there was just a beaker full of ancient swizzle sticks.

'Do you have wine? Watching my waist,' Steve said, patting his midriff.

Dad scratched his nose, feeling uncomfortable. Men shouldn't discuss their bodies in the way women did.

'Joan, do we have wine? For Steve?'

'No, you know we don't have wine,' Mum shouted, the noise of the electric carving knife starting up. Dad disappeared into the kitchen.

'Your mum bought this,' he said, returning with a dark green bottle of fizzy apple juice.

'I'll go and get some Dad,' I said. 'The supermarket's open on Sundays.' Already I was planning how Steve and I could have a smoke, maybe slip in a drink at the pub.

'That's sorted then,' Dad said. Steve waited while I lingered to see if Dad would dip into his pocket, but of course he didn't, the old bean-counter. I shouted to Mum that I was going to the supermarket, did she want anything? Then Mum called Dad into the kitchen, and they had a low discussion, until he was forced to come back with a ten-pound note.

'Get a receipt,' he said, then stepped a fraction closer. As if it were a casual afterthought, he added, 'If there's enough change, get a bottle of red too.'

'Don't be long!' Mum called.

We enjoyed our smoke in the weak winter sun. A few autumn leaves were curled on the pavements. The pub was too busy, so we went straight to the supermarket. Standing back, I watched Steve find the barcodes on the wine bottles – two for lunch and two for later – scanning them until they beeped. I checked around to see if any customers were watching us in our smart clothes.

By the time we got back, the vegetables were in their terrines and Mum had cracked the window. I told Steve to sit opposite at the table, then helped Mum as we brought in the roast potatoes, boiled potatoes (Dad), Paxo stuffing, sprouts, peas, carrots, cauliflower cheese, pigs in blankets, pigs without blankets (Dad), a large Yorkshire pudding sliced into rectangles and a jug of gravy. Lastly, Mum brought in the turkey covered in copious sheets of foil, as if we were well off.

'Wine, Joan?' Dad said, positioning his red so in a straight line with the white. Then he brushed his nose, and I'm sure I saw his Adam's apple drop with a gulp.

'Not for me,' she said, and I knew what it was she was thinking, how she didn't need it, when he did. She did not look up, instead she leant over to place her glass on the sideboard.

'Are you having red Steve?' Dad said.

'White for me,' he replied.

'I find I can take it or leave it,' Mum said to Steve. 'With or without, I'm always up on the dancefloor first. I bet you're the same. I hear you roller skate?'

Mum passed him the sprouts and he dished a single one onto his plate. 'Roller blade, yes. But I'm not very good.'

'It's the risk you take for fun, isn't it? So, do you live alone?'

'I live with my partner.'

'Oh,' Dad said, pouring gravy over his turkey. 'You run a business, alongside flying?'

'No, he's . . .my boyfriend, partner.'

'I had this friend once at work, he liked dancing,' Mum said, flopping a slice of oily Yorkshire pudding to her plate. 'I don't know what happened to him. He just disappeared. But he could really move.'

'HIV,' I said, knowing what I was doing.

'No,' Mum said. 'Don't.'

'I haven't got a knife,' Dad said.

'What?' Mum said.

'There's no knife here.' Dad gestured at the space where his knife should've been.

He waited while Mum hurried to the kitchen and I stared, then made a sorry-for-all-this face at Steve. When she returned, she turned the blade toward herself, then placed it halfway along the table, so he had to reach for it.

I filled up the glasses.

'Can I get you some water Mum?'

'No, thanks. It'll fill me up. And we've got pudding.'

I found myself looking at Dad chewing. Knowing he sensed my gaze, he never returned it. It was a routine rebuttal. While we chatted on, Mum clocked Dad each time he topped up his glass, and I wondered if Steve noticed this too.

After the knives and forks were placed together, Mum cleared the table. Dad had control over the atmosphere, however much we tried to bring in interesting airline stories.

'What's next Joanie?' he asked, a rare beam on his face.

Mum returned with a jug of custard, wiping the spout then sucking her finger. She lifted her cracker to Steve, and I watched as they tugged back and forth. He pulled softly, to give her the best chance. My God, he was a kind man.

There was a loud snap, then a waft of gunpowder as something flew across the table. Mum found a red fish which would read the emotional heat coming from her palm. I gave Steve a quick smile, then Dad and I pulled ours, him winning a spinning top. Steve leant to the floor and found a tiny notepad, which he put by my placemat.

'Those were the luxury crackers,' Mum said. 'You can tell, can't you? I went off piste this year since you'll be away. There'll only be us at Christmas. Your sister's going to her in-laws. It won't be the same. Will it?'

'I don't see the point in bothering,' Dad mumbled.

'Where will you be Steve?' Mum said.

'Caracas.' Steve glanced across at me.

'Oh, yes,' she said. 'You both have the same trip. It doesn't always work out I hear.'

'No, we were lucky,' Steve said.

'You must be excited,' Mum enthused.

'You can come when I get my travel concessions,' I assured her, with a pang of guilt crowding in.

'Would you like to travel, Jeff?' Steve asked.

'Not really. Apart from Spain,' he said. 'That's as far as I'll go. The rest is . . .' he searched for a word. 'Too far.'

'Not even the States?' I said.

'Why would I want to go there?' he said. 'Phony people.'

And I thought of all the world he would not see, and all the different airs he would not breathe.

Into the diminished global outlook, Mum brought pudding. Microwaved mince pies, apple crumble, steamed pudding, lemon meringue pie and the gravy jug, now full of heavy cream. Everything had been defrosted overnight. She would've written a list with timings on the yellow stick-it pad she kept by the phone. I knew her actions so well, it was as if I were always with her.

Dad poured the last of the red into his glass. Mum brought in a plate of Cheddar and Stilton with a few grapes the way he liked them, pre-plucked. A jar of silverskin pickled onions followed with cream crackers, because of the diabetes.

'Shall we have a bit of that Port Dad?' I suggested, slicing Cheddar from the block with the special curled knife. I had drunk enough now to feel softer, less worried by him.

He flicked the spinning wheel across the tablecloth. 'I don't think I'll open it yet.'

'Huh,' I let out a laugh without meaning to.

'We'll keep it for Christmas proper.'

Mum's eyes fixed on Dad as he leant back, creaking his chair.

'But there is that Martini,' he said. 'Your mother's not going to drink it. Steve?'

'I'm OK. But thanks.'

'Just open the Port, Jeff.'

Dad's eyes swivelled at Mum, then dropped.

'Just open it.'

I looked down at my hands, willing it to be over. Pushing back his chair, Dad picked up his glass and walked out of the door into the kitchen. He placed his glass on the side, and we listened as he went up the creaking stairs. Reaching across, Mum swung the Port onto the table, placing it in front of me with a thump.

'There,' she said. 'Open it will you?'

We heard a click as Dad shut the toilet door.

'I think we might go soon, Mum,' I said, a stammer in my voice. The Port wasn't just about Dad, it was about me too. She'd watched as I filled up my glass over and over. She didn't say anything, she didn't need to.

'Got an early start tomorrow. Orlando night stop.'

'America,' she said, breathing out. 'I nearly forgot; you haven't had your presents. I got you both a small something. Nothing much.'

Without Dad reappearing, Mum brought in two Christmas stockings she would've got from Woolworths or British Home Stores.

'Take them with you. Or open them tonight if you like. You know me, I'm easy-going. The rules are out the window this year,' she said, with no particular feeling.

Mine was an oversized brushed cotton sock with fur trimming, packed with small, wrapped objects I could easily fit in my case for Venezuela. Of course I would see Mum before Christmas, but she must've wanted to deliver them to us together, as if Steve were now part of the family. His stocking was a smaller version and when I glanced inside, his objects were unwrapped to mark the difference in our family status.

By the front door, Mum handed over the uneaten mince pies, then pushed the Port bottle into my stocking.

We lit cigarettes as soon as we were away, breathing in deeply, walking fast. Back at my flat, with the sofa folded out, we drank guilt-free amounts on the bed. Vodka from the fridge, port served in my gran's old sherry schooners. The more we drank, the more the day was left behind and so we became us again. Steve pulled out his gifts and balanced ear buds and the netted bag of chocolate coins on top of a cooling eyeshade.

'Sorry about my dad,' I said.

'Bless your mum though,' Steve said.

'I know,' I said. 'She likes you, I can tell.'

'I love her already,' he said, lighting two cigarettes, then passing me one. On the gift tag, as always, Dad hadn't written his part and Mum hadn't bothered faking his handwriting. Though for the first time she had tried out an unfamiliar word, *hugs*. Holding the gift tag to the light, I studied Mum's small print. French companies analysed handwriting to assess interview candidates, in order to weed out unreliable personalities. The circle in Mum's 'g' was different to the other letters, wide like a ship's porthole. Maybe the pen had slipped, but I suspected she was entrusting Steve, via secret code, with the idea there was an abroad version to her.

It became clear I had to live out an unlived part of Mum's life for her. I was willing to do this – though as a good daughter did I really have the choice? Was there such a thing as autonomy or energy to determine my own dreams, when they seemed so in reaction to hers?

CHAPTER 4

Autopilot

GRU – GIG – GRU

Just before my midnight, eight hours behind London, I was trying my first cigar in the Havana Club bar at the Renaissance Hotel, Sao Paulo. The soggy tip filled my mouth and the end crackled, the fumes catching my lungs. Steve rubbed between my shoulders then took hold of the cigar. The taste was bad, like a first cigarette bad, but we were in it together and determined to smoke it down to the stub.

It was New Year's Eve and the beginning of the new millennium. I thought of it as a clean slate, though doom-mongers believed the world would end at the stroke of midnight via a computer bug: planes would fall out of the sky, chaos would ensue – but it hadn't happened anywhere as far as I knew and I hoped the pessimists would be proven to be what they were, conspiracy theorists.

The Havana Club bar was luxurious. Our spot was in a velvet plum banquette curved around a small Art Deco-inspired table. Long mirrors and crystal lights echoed the modernist design of the hotel and the lavishness made me realise how well the airline must be doing, to put us up in a hotel like this.

We had arrived in Brazil three days back. Steve and I had formed a trio with another steward named Paco. On our second day we worked the shuttle from Sao Paulo to Rio, where we stayed at the Sheraton Grande. If you craned your neck from the pool deck, there were views of Ipanema. Warned by the captain about local crime, we still went out to a nightclub. Paco spoke Spanish, which he said Brazilians understood, as long as he talked with a certain speed. I wondered if French would work but decided not to try. Within an hour of arriving at the nightclub, I'd become pale and overly drunk. It turned out I'd had my drink spiked, and a man had led me outside. Luckily, I'd still got my wits enough about me to get rid of him, but then I'd slept for a good fourteen hours, not hearing Steve's phone calls and was allowed to sit in crew rest for the flight back to Sao Paulo. I was worried I wouldn't be up to going out tonight, of all nights.

I was nearly eighty percent right but was going to take things steady, which we all knew wouldn't happen. We needed to have a good pace for everything to work. A tall woman with tousled honey-brown hair and perfect posture played 'Girl from Ipanema' on the piano. Her long powerful hands were transfixing, as was the delicate low-cut sequined strappy dress. The crew at our table were fascinated by her pert breasts and kept breaking off from the conversation to examine her.

'Is it a man?' they asked.

'It's a woman,' they sniggered, as if their views were compulsory.

I sipped the Caipirinha and replaced the glass heavily, spilling it on the table. *Both*, I thought. *Surely people can be plural.*

'Careful,' Steve said.

'I am,' I said.

'You alright?'

Closing my eyes, I ran my finger over my glass while the pianist played on. So much of a person's identity could be manipulated. I'd worked out at art college how women were born female, and the rest was drag or learnt behaviour. Was it Ru Paul who'd said this? When I'd performed as a drag queen, I'd realised how even this world was for men. But women were expected to drag up every day for men. Surely I could wear make up without it being for a man? I liked my eyelashes defined, otherwise I had the face of a bleary-eyed woodland creature. Surely there was space where I could be my own audience without feeling uncomfortable?

Simone de Beauvoir wrote, 'one is not born, but rather becomes a woman.' How could I demonstrate my inner world through outside hair and clothes? Was this even possible? Everyone was malleable, but now I was a stewardess I was paid to appear a certain way whether I felt like it or not.

I knew I had to write this down. Tonight we were about to move into the twenty-first century and I needed to be prepared. My eyes darted for a waiter. As I shifted over to search for staff, for paper and pen, Steve put his hand on my knee.

'Come here,' he said, pulling me close. 'Gorgeous.'

Why he said this at this particular moment I wasn't sure, but it was distracting and so we began swaying to the music. Then I ripped a layer of paper off a drinks coaster and slipped it into my bra, as a reminder to keep these thoughts close.

As the Brazilian midnight crept closer there was confusion about how many minutes were left. The captain took out his mobile and flipped his wrist to check against his watch. Then another crew piled into the bar. Counting nine women and five men, even out of uniform I could tell them a mile off. My eye stopped on a particular woman because of her short, bleached hair. Unusually, she was wearing khaki army trousers and a silver sequin top, the back held together with criss-cross laces. I took a long gulp from my cocktail while I watched her brown swimmer shoulders. She was that rare alchemy of femme and butch. The bar began to glow, the lights tinting the atmosphere and the piano grew louder, the chords thrumming in my ears and chest.

The new crew disappeared round the other side of the bar. We crews rarely mixed, as we stuck to our own make-shift family. More cocktails arrived at the table, courtesy of the captain and the dirty glasses were whipped away as if they'd never happened. No one needed to keep score. Not tonight of all nights.

Though I missed the certainty of Big Ben's chimes, soon enough there were cheers and swirling sparklers as a lively samba started. Waiters appeared with trays of red drinks with thick slices of orange. *Happy New Year!* We'd made it. There was no blackout. The end of the world had not happened. Steve got me into an all-encompassing hug, then Paco pressed himself against our backs, and the crew

84

surrounded us in a bigger bundle of affection and kisses. Then we all drew back, separating out to form a wide circle. Crossing arms we grabbed one another's hands, singing 'Auld Lang Syne', which no one knew all the words to, but still, it didn't matter as we jigged back and forth. The other tourists in the bar rose from their individual tables, sophisticated South American men and women with refined hairstyles and chiselled chins. They raised their glasses, sipped, then moved onto the dance floor, pressing together and round us.

I danced for half an hour or so, until the adrenaline bottomed out. A jazz chanteuse began performing Portuguese songs in a low rasping voice. I would've stayed, as it was rare we ever got any real culture, but Steve and Paco wanted to search out a gay club. So, we said our farewells, and I made sure to cross round the bar to see if the woman with the silver top was still there. She was, in the centre of her crew, stubbing out a cigarette. I moved quickly off, away from her big, cow-like eyes which didn't seem to notice me.

We left the hotel into the warm night. An illuminated green cross of a pharmacy announced the temperature as 21C. The cracked, uneven pavements took us down the hill, and we got lost for a while in the unmarked streets until Paco pointed out a café with a rainbow flag in the window. Inside were revellers, brightly lit by fluorescent strip-lighting. The space inside was taken so Paco pushed his way to speak to the barmaid, while Steve and I smoked.

The gay venues in Brazil often changed, and Paco was trying to find out where to go. The crowd inside the café were shouting and jumping to the music. No one had a drink in their hand, they didn't seem to need it. So many people across the world were like this, I'd noticed. I couldn't recall the last time I'd been able to dance without it. Paco shouted loudly, '*feliz ano novo!*' and I repeated it, imitating the accent, wanting to know how to move my tongue in a Brazilian way, as if it were more important than English.

By the time we found the club, there was a short queue of men in vest tops outside. A light film of sweat covered my face, and I badly needed the toilet. Once we were in, the club was disappointingly tiny with no cages containing half-naked dancers, or rubber flapped entrances to dark rooms. There were no women, and it smelt like poppers and dank face cloths. We found a short rat-like man at a table by the door, and he handed us each a card, squiggled his pen in the air, then pointed at the bartender. It fell into place, how he would then mark your card, so no money changed hands. This was because of corruption, I presumed, and Paco explained the cashier would tally up the drinks at the end of the night. 'Don't lose it,' he said. 'Or they'll charge you big bucks.'

I pushed through the crowd to the toilet, which was a silver urinal with one lone cubicle with the door removed. The room smelt of caustic lemon from the blocks left in the troughs. As I squatted over the bowl, searching for loo paper, I watched the back of a man as he pissed into the trench. Men knew to ignore me. They didn't even register us women. This felt like freedom, no ogling making me aware of my breasts or exposed thighs. After, I found a tiny sink on the wall; when I pressed the tap it released one drip, so I wet my hands as best as I could.

I drank for a bit, running my eye over the crush for the sign of a woman. When a good dance track came on Steve, Paco and I moved onto the dancefloor and lifted our arms into the swirling lights. Steve and Paco rubbed each other's crotches with their hips and held onto the backs of each other's jeans. The local men were all tanned and muscular. They oozed easy sex, and I could tell Paco was getting more attention than Steve because he looked more like them. This made me worry, that they saw Steve as a pale string-bean of an Englishman when he was just as good as them. Then a light caught my eye. It was the bleach-haired stewardess pushing through the throng, along with two other stewards from the bar.

Before long, I began to edge over. I'd drunk enough and soon I was behind her. It took a while for her to receive my psychic chant, but when she turned, I did a little wave. Then she stood next to me and almost immediately we were shouting over the music; some words I got, and others I invented from the way her face moved. Sharon was her name. Born in Croydon, she now lived in Crystal Palace. We'd both been crossing the globe unaware we lived twenty minutes from one another. She knew of only two other lesbians working for the airline, a couple, one of whom refused to be out about it.

Maybe all of this forced something between us which might not have happened in another lifetime, but her hand soon gently rested on my back. Then we ordered shots. Black Sambuca, as thick as lovely cough medicine. We drank vodka and soda over ice with fresh lime. To rehydrate in between the proper drinks, we ordered beer.

It was while we were dancing, she kissed me. She closed her eyes and moved in. Electricity ran through me, flipping and curling, setting up novel places. We then made up a salsa dance, interlacing fingers. Later in a corner, we kissed with animal tongues; I left the rest of the world behind.

When the house lights came on at the end, it revealed

a black painted room with a skewed air conditioning unit hanging on scratch-marked walls. Sharon had lipstick smudged round her mouth, so I wiped it off with my thumb. We paid our bills and leant against the wall out front watching for Steve and Paco. When they arrived, we wound back through the streets, stumbling and shrieking. Because of Steve's accident-prone nature I pointed out the larger holes in the pavements, but still he managed to trip up the pavement.

It took an age to get back to the hotel because the streets all looked the same. Under a patch of ochre streetlight, we stopped for hot dogs out the back of a van. The vendor squeezed on mayonnaise, mustard, and just when we thought it would topple, a large spoonful of mashed potato and fried onion.

We ate them greedily. Our hands sticky, meaty, sexy. Steve and Paco went ahead. I could tell something was probably imminent between them. Once we were alone again, Sharon pressed me against the front of a car. I kept one eye open for the risk of men, until desire outweighed the danger. The metal of the car bonnet buckled as she pushed me down more intensely. Her lips were so plump, all I wanted to do was bite them, the world edible. Ours. When she lifted away, I saw the street anew and I wondered if this was love, because it felt very much like love.

The early morning sky barely had stars. The outlines of buildings began to solidify.

'Your eyes are so . . .' I said and she made a funny face, so I pressed my lips together, resisting the urge to say something more.

'Let's head back, babe,' she said, and I glanced to see if she were using 'babe' satirically, impersonating a cockney from a pub, but she wasn't. This was her actual accent and I realised I hadn't heard her voice until now.

To squeeze the last drop out of the night we decided on the café across from the hotel. Inside, the smell of coffee switched on my brain. Small, folded pies with crimped edges sat under glass on the countertop while a bulky juice machine churned, on top a stack of oranges ready. I watched a man order a pile of dough balls. He didn't pay, but just sat down, so I figured it was a European type arrangement where they trust you not to do a runner. When it was my turn, I said '*dos cafes*' and then pointed at the dough balls, hoping my poor Spanish might deputise for my non-existent Portugese. Then I tried '*quatre*' and when the server shook her head, I held up four fingers.

We sat in the corner, my knee against Sharon's under the table. Between my legs I felt a fulness, like a tulip flower ready to open. The waitress brought the coffee in thick brown earthenware cups and saucers. The foreignness was exciting, so I slotted my finger into the tiny handle to enjoy the design. The dough balls had a soft cheesy interior the texture of choux pastry. My heart drummed hard from the coffee, and café clientele arrived with clean styled hair and shiny washed ears, kissing one another in the new year. When an outlandishly fluffy dog began to yap, we paid and headed back to the hotel.

'So, your room or mine?' she said, pressing the elevator button.

This was really happening.

'Yours?' I needed my room free to rest before the flight later today. In the elevator, on one of the brushed suede wall panels, someone had left a print of a bare backside. We knew it would've been a drunk crew member. A comrade in partying, the message said, *we'll always be free when drunk*. I could tell from the delight on Sharon's face we both got it.

A floor above mine, Sharon's room had an identical configuration of writing desk on the left, bed on the right, armchair and pouffe in front of the curtains.

'Do you want another drink?' she said.

'I'm not sure I can,' I said.

'Go on, I'm going to have one.'

'OK then.'

'So what little friends do we have in here?' She knelt in front of the mini bar. Running her forefinger over the miniatures in the door, she chucked one over.

'Hang the cost,' she said.

Even though I'd clasped my hands together to catch it, it landed on the floor. I felt adolescent. Physical coordination was linked to sexual prowess, but I never could catch. Tough, fierce girls were better between the sheets. Everyone supposed this. Girls who went on top and as well as underneath and back to front, who yelled, free, abandoned, they were the sporty ones.

'Cognac *con hielo*,' I said, studying the bottle.

'What's that?'

'Brandy with ice,' I said, deciding not to tell her about Dad.

There was a piece of paper stuck over the lid with small, printed numbers to show it was a registered brand. Snap! I twisted off the lid, then downed half, wincing at the burn. I had never bought anything from a hotel mini bar, inflated prices, especially when we got it free from the aircraft. Sharon was chucking it about like she was made of money.

On the bed, me against the pillows, she climbed beside me. She made the slightest movement closer, then began kissing my neck, my lips, while my hands tried to find where the criss-cross laces on her top began. To feel wanted, and safe in feeling wanted – this was it. The very truth in being with another woman cancelled out every other thing. There was no floating out of my body now, no dreaming of a life. This was all I wanted. I tugged at the strings of her top, as cack-handed as a teenage boy trying to undo a bra.

'Here,' she said, and pulling a small knot, started to shake it off. Her nipples were wide and dark, like grown up women's breasts. Mothers, I tried not to think of mothers. I ran my hands over her ribs towards her jeans. Her nipples began to shrink into points. We were girls and yet also supposed to be women. But there had been a delay, I was sure. Arrested development because of the laws. Then she pushed me back on the bed while tugging at my trousers, and we pressed together. I pulled off my top, discarding the piece of ripped paper from my bra. Skin on skin. I had forgotten quite how like a whole universe a woman's body was. An open door, there was enough to explore for a lifetime, and I wondered what the world might be like if Christopher Columbus had just stayed at home with a beautiful woman. Whether man would have needed to plant a flag in the moon and claim it as found.

We kissed. Worried she wouldn't think I was active enough, I sucked then bit her nipple.

'Fuck,' she said.

'Sorry. Did that hurt?'

'No, it felt *good*.'

I crouched over, kissing her stomach, while I drew down on my haunches.

'What do you want me to do?'

'Bad things,' she said. Even though I still had bobbed hair, I wanted her to realise I had some savagery, so I stared at her hard in the eyes, while unbuttoning her trousers.

A menu of options rolled through my mind. I decided on aiming towards stimulating her G-spot. I had come to think of this as a small patch of internal soft-land. An area so smooth, it was mousse-like compared to other parts of the vagina. Still some women believed it was mythical, but I'd read an article and discovered mine during an eleven-day trip to Lusaka.

By the way she was sounding, I was getting close. Still it took time, and my mind began to drift forward to my next trip. When she went quiet, I nearly stopped, my arm ached, but then she shuddered, and let out an almighty cry as if a volt had shot through her. She pulled me to her, then gripped her legs around my hips, holding on tight. It was a wonderful thing to be able to do.

We stayed like this for a while. Clasped. Unmoveable. Her letting out a gentle sob. Me listening for a change in her breathing.

'I didn't mean to be a big baby,' she said, wiping her cheek.

I saw her head going down between my legs and wondered how many other women she had done this with. Too drunk, the sensitivity around my clitoris was somewhere off in a side room. I wanted to go back to the kissing we'd done on the car. White dots floated around my vision. It was no good; I shook her shoulder. When she moved off, I edged myself up against the headboard.

'Sorry,' I said. 'Probably need some sleep.'

She shifted to the end of the bed. Bending over so I could see the nodules of her spine, she opened the mini bar.

This time she took out two vodkas from the top shelf. She gestured one towards me, but I shook my head. The alarm clock said ten, I had to be in my uniform at five p.m.

I didn't know what I expected to happen, or why I didn't just leave, but soon Sharon was in the shower. I pulled the duvet, then smoothed it flat. Going around the room, I collected my clothes and found my room key. Pick up was no longer a distant obligation. Sharon wouldn't leave until tomorrow, she had time to sleep it all off and have one clear hangover free day, whereas I didn't have the luxury. Getting dressed in last night's smoky clothes, I couldn't wait to get to shower in my own room. I opened her curtains. The sun was on the skyscrapers, the distant hills lost in a haze.

After a while, she appeared in a white dressing gown with the collars pulled up to her ears. Her hair was wrapped in a towel and she appeared impish and young. Her beauty came from her high cheek bones, her lashes like small brushes.

'It was a good night, wasn't it?' I said.

She stood, waiting by the bathroom door. 'Yes, it was.'

Pausing, she glimpsed about the room as if she'd just come to. 'Have a safe flight home won't you.' There was no *I'll see you again*, or *you've given me the best time of my life*.

'I guess I'll see you about,' I said, resting my hand on the door handle.

'Great,' she said.

So, that was it. I clicked the door behind me and took the lift to my room. At any point, a crew member could open their door and see me carrying my shoes, or worse, I would bump into the captain who would smell the brandy, the sex, and with less than eight hours to call.

But I was not caught. Back in the cleanly made-up room,

I set my alarm, took a hot shower, then crawled under the cool sheets. Sleep would heal, as always. I drifted, picturing my body letting in the mini army of workers dressed in hard hats, ready to work double-time on my repair. They would flush out the pipes, rinse my organs, brush out the sweat and sulphurous wind. Like a dirty city whose streets got invisibly washed by night, my team had never failed me so far.

I slept for five hours, until the wakeup call drilled the bedside phone. Then I did what I always did, picked up the phone with an alert voice. The receptionist thanked me for staying at *The Renaissance Hotel*, which reassured me I wasn't in trouble.

One hour until pick up, I'd already packed and ironed my shirt, because I knew I wasn't to be trusted. I checked under the bed, more for mental stability than lost objects. In the bathroom I collected the small bottles, zipped them in my suitcase for Mum.

Thirty minutes before pick up, I drank the last of the bottled water and got the jumpy feeling before re-joining the crew. As I left the room I gave myself a moment to try to understand the source of the panic. Drawing a blank, I put it down to hangover.

In the foyer, there was a cordoned off airline area with the complimentary soft drinks. I positioned my luggage by a small armchair with a view of the lift, then poured myself black coffee and dropped a cellophaned lemon cake in my bag. Before the crew arrived, I took out a hotel notepad and wrote down the words *female identity* with two question marks. The crew flowed from the lift, one after the next, never Sharon, however much I wanted it. How polished we became with our pressed shirts, clean fastened hair and shined shoes. Whether we'd seen one another naked or vomiting in a bush, all indiscretions were wiped clean.

When Steve arrived, he appeared bright-eyed.

'Fag my sweet?' he said, pulling out cigarettes.

'No, I'm alright.'

He returned the packet to inside his jacket. There was no smoking in uniform, and he would have to go outside for one. He leant forward.

'Me and Paco had sex,' he whispered.

I was obliged to ask, 'Did you like it?'

'He was nice. But after, he went out to buy coconut water. I didn't want him to come back, but he did, and he stayed for ages, sitting on the bed. It took an age to get rid of him. He kept saying how he really liked me.'

'Don't you like him?'

'I'm not sure. It was funny, you know.' He pointed to his trousers. I nodded, frowning. I didn't know and the coarse side of Steve made me feel at odds with him. It didn't match his sweetness. It crossed my mind there was an element of him going through with it, just so he could tell me the story. I didn't say anything about Sharon; I was still hoping for her to run out of the lift.

I had never been the type of woman who could have sex with someone and not want a relationship. For some reason, as gay women, we'd been told we should be able to do this so we could equal gay men. Many women could, I just wasn't one of them. As the coach pulled up outside the hotel, there was still no Sharon. A series of clicks came from wheelie handles as the crew shifted out front towards the forecourt.

It was nine o'clock in the evening local time, and I milled round the back of the coach, watching the driver pack the suitcases. Just as I handed over my luggage, I heard my name and turned to find Sharon striding out in skin-tight blue jeans and a gold lame stretch vest. No bra, her nipples were pressing out through the material. I noticed the driver staring.

'I made it. Just wanted to give you this,' she said, taking my hand and pushing paper into it. She leant forward, smelling of strong alcohol, and said, 'There's something there for you.'

Her pupils were wide dark holes. I peered at the rectangular piece of paper, folded like a wrap of cocaine. Feeling hot, I motioned at the coach, shaking my head. How could she think this was alright when I was about to head towards airport security? In South America?

'What is it?' I said, offering it back.

'Just a memento.'

Standing close, she closed my fingers round it. It must have appeared to Steve that we couldn't stop holding hands.

'Enjoy your night,' I said. 'I've got to go.'

She nodded, a quick smile moving onto her face.

'Nice dimples' was all I could think of to say. As I turned, I sensed the crew watching. The heat of the night prickled where the rim of my hat met my forehead. I pulled myself up the coach steps, and feeling she was inspecting my behind, clenched it.

Entering the dark interior of the coach, the crew glanced up. Steve had saved me a space at the back and along with Paco, they jeered like schoolchildren. I slumped down in a double seat in front and removed my hat, tucking Sharon's gift into an inside pocket.

'So?' Steve said, poking his head above the seats. Still, I kept quiet and as the coach pulled away, I turned to see a shrinking Sharon, now joined by one of her crew, lighting her cigarette, cupping his hands to her face.

The coach passed avenues, parks, and a modernist museum structure. Couples with small dogs strolled into their evening. I felt bitter towards the flight ahead. Sharon would be out drinking, she might have sex with another woman, which would erase the memory of me. Soon we had passed from Paulista Avenue into the dimly lit *favelas*. We had been warned not to go out here. I could see the lights go on forever, a whole established town of slum living.

From my pocket I pulled out Sharon's gift, praying it wasn't drugs. If it was, I would simply tuck it in the crease between the seats and wash my hands before going through security. But as I opened it inside I found a piece of card folded in two covered in pencil marks. The drinks tally from the nightclub. It was Sharon's card, denoting fourteen drinks in all. I blushed both at the volume and how she'd saved this memento for me. On the back was her name and phone number. Beneath this, one single X.

A few weeks later I spent my birthday with Steve at a restaurant with white tablecloths, and in the same week I asked Sharon to be my girlfriend. A small miracle, she'd said yes.

On Valentine's day, I was in Dallas for a night stop. My room was on the 24th floor of the Adam's Mark convention hotel. It had scuffed wallpaper and a crack in the tiles on the bathroom floor. Still, there were the usual two king-sized beds and dark wooden desk with ink blotter paper, free envelopes and notepaper. On the flight over an Irish woman had got drunk and held my arm in the galley as she pleaded for more wine. She told me her brother had just died, and her husband had served divorce papers just before her 60th birthday. I felt sorry for her and had done the old wipe the alcohol round the glass trick, finally getting her back to her seat with a cup of strong sugary tea. The US had become stricter about drunk passengers. There had been more and more incidents of abused cabin crew, and so now ground staff no longer tolerated drunk passengers on arrival. I wondered if this signalled a sea change, a more sober wind coming in.

On the flight over I had also decided to try something new on take-off. These days I got to choose my position and so therefore chose to work on the upper deck. Now my body was aflame I wanted to see if the run up to take-off, all that shuddering down the runway, could be made more thrilling by inserting a pair of love eggs. Apparently, it could induce an orgasm without me touching anything, and since I was getting better at controlling my face, masking my true feelings, I thought I should give it a go. It had turned out rather uneventful, but still it livened up what was to be a particularly uneventful flight.

Sharon was at The Stamford, Singapore, fourteen hours ahead, which meant she was living half a day ahead of mine. My morning was her evening, and because of this, it felt oppressive, like there was too much time to my day without her.

I showered and, disappointed by the lack of dressing gown, sat on the bed in a towel which smelt of coffee. With the pillows propped behind, I found a comfortable position and resisted turning on the TV. The fact Sharon was so far away, while I was here, was painful and immobilising. We had joked about how one day we'd go on joint rosters, meaning we would fly together on the same trips and have the same days off. But experienced crew warned against it, saying it was cursed and broke couples up because living, working and playing with one another meant you were never apart. I knew this wouldn't suit me, but also I knew I would find it hard to say if I needed space in our new relationship. Still, it was too early to be making any real plans, but I needed something concrete to hold on to.

Dead on nine, I dialled the number of Sharon's hotel using a calling card from the hotel gift shop. It rang after a series of clicks. When the call was finally picked up, my heart pounded at the strange hybrid accent of the operator.

'Sharon Smith, please.'

'Certainly,' the voice said. 'Putting you through.'

There was a pause, before a further ringing which meant I was practically in her room.

'Hello?' she said.

'Oh, I found you,' I said, thinking how I never remembered how she sounded.

'Fuck, I miss you,' she said. 'I couldn't concentrate on the flight over. I'm sure I was shitty with a passenger.'

'Me too. I thought about you all the way.'

'We don't have long,' she said. 'So, how do you want to . . .? I've not done this before.'

I found the hotel notepad where I'd jotted down a few notes: *clothing, fingers, backs of knees, dirty words? Say, I want to fuck you hard.*

'Right,' I said. 'So . . .' I began gently. 'What are you wearing?'

'Apart from my hat, nothing,' she joked.

'Place your fingers between your legs.'

'Right,' she said.

'Now pretend it's me. Right there, behind your knees.

And you, well, you're biting my breasts. Or "titties"? Is that a better word?'

'Just stick with "tits"' she said. '"Titties" sounds like "panties" – paedo words.'

'So, imagine I'm inside you. Can you feel it?'

'Carry on,' she said. 'I can smell you. I'm with you right now.'

I could hear Sharon's breathing. Disembodied by distance, I decided I should make a noise, so I let out a sigh, then ran my hand over my belly down to the short landing strip of hair I'd formed at her request.

My hand became Sharon's hand, and the ear-piece Sharon's mouth. I must have accidentally licked the mouthpiece because I could taste perfume from a guest before me. Then I thought I heard the chambermaid with her cart pull up and how I'd forgotten to put out the DO NOT DISTURB sign.

'Are you still there?' she said.

'Sorry, yes.' I forced my mind back to her.

'Say something,' she said.

'I can feel it,' I said.

'Something more,' she said, and I pictured her room in Singapore, the beige carpet, the locked balcony which overlooked the metallic art centre on the quay. The locals had given it a nickname: dragon fruit.

'God, I'm turned on,' she said.

I heard a knocking sound.

'What was that?' I said.

Silence.

'I just came,' she said. 'I was thinking of you. On top.'

'The Telecom card will expire in sixty seconds,' came a recorded voice.

'I'll go and buy another,' I said, panicking. 'I can go right now be back in ...'

'Don't worry,' she said. 'It's late now. I've got to get down to the bar. You know ...'

'Thank you for using Delta International Calling Cards,' the voice said, with a beep. I waited before putting down the phone. A weight formed on my chest, and I found it hard to breathe. I stared at the phone, *ring me, ring me, call me back.*

In the end I forced myself off the pillows. The day ahead was flat. There was hours until lunch and Sharon would be out dancing, her sky dark with the thrill of stars. I wanted to lose this swathe of Dallas time and get back home. The stewardesses on my flight were having their nails done for five dollars. For them it was about how cheap things were compared to the UK, as if something got won every time. I liked my nails short, unpolished. Being away from home and from their partners or children for them seemed so liberating, and yet time down route for me was becoming underwhelming.

Sulking for as long as I could, without moving my limbs an inch, I thought of my friends back home. The L Gang with their teaching jobs and careers starting in television. One friend I'd met at art college was now touring Europe with a performance art group. They must think I'd lost it, lost every talent or dream I once had. I used everyone else's achievements as small sticks to poke myself with.

Eventually, I came round to an idea I should be hungry. So I took the lift down to the foyer and walked about the carpeted corridors, watching the action outside a conference room where models dressed in padded ski suit jackets and moon boots held paper cups of coffee. I slowed, eyeing up whether I might be able to sneak in for anything free they might be giving out.

Crossing the inner walkway from the hotel to the shopping mall, the low winter sun caught the smears on the glass. The Galleria was at the other end and when I reached the start, pink helium balloons filled every shop window. Stalls were selling love muffins, build-a-bear teddies holding hearts, fruit scented Yankee candles. A store assistant from Victoria's Secret came out and intruded on my personal space, asking if I wanted a consultation. I shook my head. Matching lacy bra and knickers sets were for stewardesses who dressed for men under their uniforms.

Noticing a sign for the ice rink, I walked through the mall, getting the usual zoned out feeling of nothing seeming real. In the centre of the ice was a young girl, ten or eleven, with small buds of breasts under her leotard. Skating backwards with her arms outstretched, she sped by as her chiffon mini skirt caught the breeze. From over the other side of the rink, a man studied her in the way men do without thinking about it. I tried to fathom whether he knew her, or if I needed to intervene. The young girl glided backwards and, gaining speed, she turned, then pivoted in the air. Her confidence was incredible – and as the man watched on, I imagined tapping him on the arm saying, 'I've got your number.'

The girl landed on the ice and lost her footing, then steadied herself.

'Great! One more time,' he shouted, and the girl glanced over her shoulder, her blades gliding. She nodded, then began it all again. Father and daughter probably, the loving kind, and something in me sank down. The sweet waft of cinnamon hit my nose and I followed it. From Taco Bell I ordered a burrito with pumpkin fries and from Bella Giardino, a slice of pepperoni pizza and a medium-sized diet lemonade.

When I got back to my room, I took off all my clothes, relieved to be free from waistbands. I laid the food out across the duvet, then got under the covers. Switching on the TV I found a film where a man searched for his daughter in a post-apocalyptic New York. Of course she was under the rubble all along. For some reason I couldn't stop crying, and I thought of a cool glass of wine and how I wouldn't let myself have it.

After the film finished, I tried to find something art-housey to watch. My brain was turning to mush. This life encouraged this. It was clear I was waiting for something to happen. My uniform was getting tighter. I didn't want to go to uniform stores to get a bigger size. I clicked the remote, trawling through adverts, twenty-four-hour news channels and made-for-TV movies. I told myself the hours spent in this American hotel room didn't count as real ones, not like those at home in London, or on Sharon-time. Time here felt vapid and insignificant. Why shouldn't I enjoy trashy food and light films like other people? The majority of the world lived on comforting rubbish, sleepwalking, or just getting by until their next holiday. There was a reason people didn't expect too much. It saved disappointment. I should let myself off the hook, surely. I had to stop thinking I could be different to anyone else.

CHAPTER 5

The True Film

LGW – PMI – LGW

We were both still alive and that counted for something. The hotel room was mottled in shadow as the bright day insisted on solidifying the balustrade. As I moved, my head felt packed heavy with sand and my back ached as if I'd been kicked in the kidneys. I studied Sharon's eyelids, resenting sleep for taking her away. She seemed so still, and it struck me she could've died in the night.

I held my knuckle in front of her mouth. Long seconds passed before a definite warmth brushed my hand. Only now did I notice how her nostrils appeared painted black inside. I wanted to put a finger inside these little caves. But was this how murderous thoughts began? Hovering my hand there again, I debated, what if it hadn't been her breath but heat from my own hand bouncing off her? Lifting the duvet I watched her chest for inhalation. Her breasts were now so familiar. How could someone's breasts become as everyday as furniture? I wanted them to be unknown again, thrilling. Still no movement. Could this be it? The cardiac arrest I was trained for?

I began the medical preliminaries for DR ABC

D for Danger. R – Response.

'Sharon?'

A – Airway – her mouth was all clear from the outside.

B for Breathing – she snuffled, perhaps experiencing pleasure on a far-off island. She turned over, her shark-fin shoulder blades jutting out a clear message: *Get away from me Karen. You're too much.*

She was alive. I leant over the side of the bed, then dropped forward, crawling on my hands and knees, enjoying the ability to move. There was a yellow-purple bruise on my thigh. I found my security pass and purse safe on top of my airline handbag and breathed. I was Hong Kong awake, eyes so open they felt chalked in the sockets. On the wall was a painting of a Spanish port with yachts and palm trees. PALMA DE MALLORCA. We were in Palma. How odd. As long-haul crew we would never normally fly to Europe for work. It didn't feel right, breaking the usual pattern somehow.

If only I could turn my body inside out, wire brush it, then soak it in the bathroom sink. I padded over to my wheelie bag: inside were the four porcelain airline coffee cups edged with black and white images of European cities taken from the aircraft. I remembered swinging round a lamp post and a grey cobbled pavement, how I'd run my hand over smooth silvery stones, then rested my cheek on a cool wall. Was it my legs which had gone in the air in a V-shape to loud applause? I'd performed a routine in drag not so long ago. The casino in Harare. The locals had thought me a witch, but the crew loved it. The locals had not understood my wig, or my impersonation of a drag queen. I was trying to bring back my art college routine. Last night, had there been shouting? Had I made an accusation? It felt very much like I'd said something awful. Something unforgivable to Sharon.

Butterflies in my stomach took hold. I remembered Dad back home once swinging round a lamp post before being sick over next door's car. Was I too sinful to be forgiven? The carpet would hold me through these lamp post memories if I just stayed low enough. I pressed the weave in the wool, resisting placing my cheek to it. My heart skittered and I wanted to escape my skin. I felt truly awful. Were Dad and I the same hateful person? Did I have a choice? I had to get my head together. Unified. Just be me, by myself, talking to myself kindly in a voice which sounded like mine. If only I could have one nice thought in a calm voice, like how I spoke to other people. Or a tangerine. A tangerine had all those clean fat cushions of water to it.

The floor tipped like at a fun house and before I could stop, more truth came at me, covering me in a wave of sweat. I studied Sharon, still asleep. I'd argued with her. She had stood by the bed with her hands on her hips, hadn't she, while I'd ranted about something very, very honest. Something about her ex's dog. And her ex's body. How sometimes dog-walking with an ex wasn't just that.

Taps, I thought. Water. Bathroom? There were no edges to hang on to, no safe place. If only Sharon would wake up and make the room normal. She had the power to do that, just like Mum. I would know from her mood how bad I had been. How Dad I had been.

On the floor I found a carrier bag of bottled water and crisps. In one continuous gulp, I drank a whole bottle, then crushed the air out the plastic bottle, my scalp flinching at the noise. Still, it was not enough of a disturbance to stir her. Levering myself up with the desk, I remembered the night Dad pressed his hips against the TV in the lounge. I'd just finished revising for my school exams and sped in for the start of *Dallas*. He wasn't supposed to be drinking so, caught red-handed with a can, he'd bolted out of his chair and pushed the lager down the front of his trousers. There he'd stayed, like a statue, blocking the screen. When he walked out of the room, the can pushed out against his fly like an erection. I couldn't believe what I'd seen. So much of my life consisted of me being encouraged not to react.

Embarrassed, the next morning I'd told Mum all about it. It was painful to disclose something so strange, and I hadn't expected to be believed. But Mum did, and she confronted Dad as soon as he came downstairs for work.

'Come tell your father what you saw him do last night,' she'd said. I'd not been ready to confront him face to face. I thought Mum would deal with things, as she always did. Finally, I dipped my head and said, 'You put a can in your trousers.' Instead of saying sorry, he just stood there with that beady parrot glare. After a while, he spoke, but still I didn't dare look him in the eye. 'So, you told on me then?' and I hadn't known I'd been in a contract with him, or he'd believed I was there to defend him. This was the moment I realised there were the two sides – Mum or Dad. I should've kept quiet; it should've been our secret. He might have loved me more after that.

'Where are we?' Sharon said. Turning over, elongating an arm in a stretch, her eyes puffy.

It took me a moment to return to the room.

'Spain,' I said. 'Mallorca.'

'What?' She flexed her fingers. 'Oh, I thought I was at home.'

'We brought the Arsenal football team across,' I said.

Sharon rubbed her forehead. She was hungover but didn't look bad. She found the remote from the bedside table and switched on the TV, something she always did before coming to. A disaster movie was playing, a blazing tower.

'Water,' she groaned, and I brought a bottle to the bed. She drank a few sips. We had not had sex in days. Up until this point it was something we always wanted to do, but the relationship was not at a stage where we could discuss what it meant when it didn't happen.

Sharon muted the TV, then pulled back the curtain to the hot September sun. I could see a man smoking on a roof top.

'How're you doing?' Sharon said.

'Fine,' I said, knowing I was bad.

'Do you remember being pulled off the floor?'

My face flushed. I wanted to get out of my body. The only way I knew how was to drink. I wished I hadn't topped up my glass so often. But all the crew did. Everyone wanted me to because that's when the party happened. I wanted to be well known for something, and there it was. There was no other option for the evenings but the meals, the bars, the good times ending in one way. It was my approach to being together in our funny makeshift crew family.

'Was I? You know?'

'You flashed your boobs. Then banged on about a woman called Cindy Sherman.'

'The artist. Oh. Nothing more?'

'No . . .not really. I think . . .'

There it was. The gap. The stopping of words. The cavernous pause in Sharon's usual airy vocabulary. She was holding back, too nice to say anything truthful. Everyone was too embarrassed to ever tell me what I might've done. She switched off the TV, and without it the room sank down into a lower version of itself.

'I could eat a bloody horse,' Sharon said. 'Shall we order food?'

I rushed into action. A job! Something to make amends with. I found the hotel flip folder, discovered the room service section, then ran my finger down the menu finding our favourite hotel staple – Club Sandwich served with French fries. Redemption would come if I organised this one thing. So I chose the drinks, two cans of Spanish *naranja*, thinking how I would pay for it all, a generous gesture at check out. *I'll get this*, I'd say, plucking the bill from her hand and pressing my Diners Card onto the reception desk. Sharon liked me when I was fearless. As I ordered on the phone, I could sense Sharon listening to me sounding sober and in control. At the end I remembered to say, *muchos gracias*. Relief. Last night could be shut into yesterday, now the food was coming.

Still, there was the blackout at the end of the evening. But when I thought about most journeys home these days in London or away, walking along the street from the station, finding my keys, getting the door open, flopping onto the mattress – none of these details ever got registered. Why would they? Some things were so mundane they were meant to go unnoticed. The brain didn't record everything like a video camera. Truth was, maybe what I couldn't remember about last night wasn't really worth remembering.

When the knock came Sharon ran naked from the bed and locked herself in the bathroom. This was so the waiter wouldn't know we were two women in bed together. We were forever trying to limit being fodder for men's masturbation, or suffering some remark. As I turned the handle, I heard her brushing her teeth and then the waiter came in and placed the tray on the bed. I tipped him and once he'd gone, tapped on the bathroom door. We got back into bed before lifting the metal covers from the plates. Before starting to eat, I kissed Sharon on the lips to test the temperature. From her everyday kiss, I knew I was safe.

As usual, I sorted out the condiment sachets into the ones to take home. Sharon pressed the remote and the TV screen crunched back to life and there it was – the same picture of the skyscraper on fire. She turned up the volume. I was pleased we were eating and far away from accusations about my vanished sex drive. A man spoke rapidly in Spanish. Then a small plane flew into the tower next to the one on fire. The picture shook and we realised we were watching footage taken on a video camera. A woman yelled out, then there was quiet until a woman said, 'Oh god, oh my god, I'm so sorry I screamed.'

'This isn't a film,' I said. 'This is real life?'

'See if they've got BBC World News,' Sharon said, and she began trawling through channels of tarot card readings. A sudden stab in my leg made me feel under the sheet and I found a rough scab on my knee. I held up the bedclothes and pressed round the tender bruise, saw a patch of dried blood.

Sharon eventually found an American news channel where the newsreader reported that two aircraft had flown into the World Trade Centre.

I watched for a while, then got out of bed and went to the bathroom. I sucked toothpaste from my toothbrush remembering there had once been a time when hangovers were guilt-free. Those days with the L Gang staying over, rising late, eating toast and mugs of tea, then laughing about how I'd left a trail of vodka miniatures over the dancefloor, secreted into the club via my bra-cups.

'A third plane has flown into a building in Washington,' Sharon shouted.

I busied myself by applying a plaster to my knee. So there was a disaster in America. This would certainly get me off the hook from the previous night.

'A series of hijacks. I'm going to call the CSD,' Sharon said. 'See if she knows what's going on.'

'Do you think we'll get home?' I said. I'd arranged to meet the L Gang later. Murmurs of discontent had risen, how they thought I was seeing too much of Sharon; someone had asked me if I was truly happy with her.

By the time Sharon found the briefing sheet with the room number of the on-board manager, she was wiping tears from her face. One tower had collapsed, and small ant-like figures were throwing themselves from the building. A fourth plane had flown into a field somewhere across America. We sat waiting to see if more planes were going to go down, and whether it would expand to our airline.

I handed her a tissue, but the whole thing felt far off, as if my skin were a padded jacket, and I was an imaginary voice in the lining. Only yesterday morning we'd been on standby at her flat, happy in the knowledge that, being on joint rosters, we would be called out for the same trip. We could have gone anywhere together, pot luck. It could have even been a flight to New York. Instead we flew a specially

111

chartered Boeing 777 to take the Arsenal football team
to play Palma. Sharon worked in first class with the team
directors, and I worked in business class with the footballers.
Sharon was a Crystal Palace supporter, but the game did
nothing for me. It was Dad's thing, his private time with the
telly; on a Saturday afternoon with the football he couldn't
be disturbed. Even the sound of the crowds roaring made
me feel melancholic, like something was missing.

As the football team rested, I'd made sure the blinds
were pulled down. While they dozed I'd paused by the
goalkeeper, David Seaman. He was too tall for his business
class seat and was hanging out of it. Briefly I'd held my left
hand alongside his, measuring it. His was twice the length
of mine and I realised how he must have been born to be
a goalkeeper. My body still gave no hint as to my calling.
Apart from a womb – which offered a role I didn't want –
being tall and sturdy was what I had. This was when I'd
taken the coffee cups and put them in my bag.

Sharon spoke to the CSD who said to wait for scheduling to confirm whether our flight would be cancelled. All
airports in the UK were closed and any flights not mid-air
were now grounded. There might be special dispensation
for the football team, but we would have to wait. We
wouldn't know what was happening for at least four hours,
so we went out to catch the mood in the streets.

Outside the hotel, the sound of cicadas rang out. It was
three in the afternoon. A man sat at a café, stirring sugar
into an espresso, reading a newspaper. It would be yesterday's news, when everything was stable. No one here
appeared moved by the disaster. I had expected people
milling around, talking loudly, gesticulating.

Finding a quiet bar we sat out on the terrace. Last night,

while we were getting drunk in a restaurant, hijackers were planning to take over planes. A spoon dropped and I flinched. When the waiter arrived, I pretended to be contemplating the menu as if I didn't know what I wanted. Delaying ordering a Bloody Mary straight off, Sharon stared at me over the table. If we were going to operate home, we would be picked up in four hours. We were supposed to have a minimum of eight hours without drinking before a flight.

'Bloody Mary,' I said.

The waiter nodded.

'Coke,' Sharon said. I studied my fingers full of pins and needles. That old, submerged feeling of the sadness of drinking alone smothered my chest. As my heart pounded on, my hands shook so much I put them under the table.

'Fuck it. We're in shock,' Sharon said. 'A drink will sort it.' So she called back the waiter and ordered the same.

'I think I'm going to be sick,' I said, tasting bile at the back of my throat. I wanted to call Mum, tell her I loved her, in case something happened, but she didn't like the word 'love'. Too strong, but what other words were there? I'm very fond of you, Mum. She liked greeting cards with the words already printed but I always insisted on drawing my own cards for her.

Checking the solidity of the table leg with my foot, I pulled out a thin paper napkin from the silver holder and pressed it to my lips. The waiter arrived and placed down our drinks, leaving a bowl of salted peanuts between us. As I drank down the spicy red juice, I lodged the ice between my teeth and crunched it. Sharon motioned for me to wipe the sides of my mouth.

'People are so mental aren't they,' Sharon said. 'Fucking idiots.'

I agreed, glad it wasn't me who was the idiot. We sat waiting under the cloudless sky made bluer by the white-washed walls. The cicadas fell silent. A delivery man wheeled a trolley up stacked with red crates. The waiter stood chatting to him, having a cigarette, before helping him with the bottles.

'The same again,' I called over to the waiter, swivelling my finger in the air like I'd watched Dad do countless times. He heard me and nodded.

'Is that wise?' Sharon said.

'Isn't this what the end of the world might be like?' I said. The first time I had seen Dad swivel his finger was on the plane to Spain. To Mallorca, in fact, this very island. Our hotel had been vast, on a cliff top overlooking the beach. It had a downstairs disco and a dinner buffet with troughs of chips and veal floating in oil. Nothing like this part, Palma, with its thin streets and smart leather shoe shops, and our polite peanuts and steady Bloody Marys.

During the second drink, with the third on order, a soft calm came over us. Enough so I could ask Sharon what I really wanted to know.

'So,' I said, 'What *exactly* happened last night?'

'Well, you were funny as usual,' she said.

Good news: I studied the light on the opposite building, the blue doors painted so fresh. I had permission to enjoy my life guilt free again. Sharon shifted in her seat and peeled the top off a cardboard coaster. I knew the satisfaction in doing this, managing one intact perfect layer.

'At first, like usual, everything was brilliant . . .' she said.

My stomach flipped, my eyes darting to my hands.

'But there came a point when you weren't making any sense.'

'Right.' There was a tickle against my leg. I looked under the table to find an ant. I flicked it to the floor, squashing it, immediately regretting it. It wasn't like me to kill a living thing. Since art college I'd believed in reincarnation.

'You frightened me,' she added, looking away.

It was here I should've apologised, or asked how, but instead I sat very still, avoiding her face.

'And I do not fancy my ex,' she said. 'A dog-walk *can* just be a dog-walk.'

The waiter returned with the last round.

'Yes. What a terrible disaster,' I said, changing the subject. 'Those poor crew members.'

CHAPTER 6

Happy Hour

LGW – IAH – LGW

It was a Southern spring day with quick sun from clear skies when the plane landed into George Bush International. This was my thirty-sixth trip to Texas since I'd begun flying and the first time I was going to attempt something different. Today, I was without Sharon. We'd come off joint rosters after she said she needed space and 'time to redefine her boundaries', which was a line straight out of Oprah. Steve had stopped asking me about her some time back; I think he mistrusted her and felt possessive over me. One night he took my mobile and hid it in one of his kitchen cupboards, saying I needed to be in the same room when with him; that she wasn't worth all the worry.

After 9/11 I'd been waiting to be scheduled something, anything, and I would've been grateful for a measly paid night stop at the dreaded Sheraton in Lagos, with its bedbugs and sex workers in the bar. Money was short. Our rosters had been filled with endless 24-hour standby days, and we'd been offered as much unpaid leave as we wanted.

On the brief journey from the airport to the hotel, I sat near the back of the coach, hoping the crew wouldn't ask what I had planned for the rest of the day. After last time, I wanted to avoid anything to do with 'Happy Hour' at the Houston Marriot North.

Along the highway we passed the National Museum of Funeral History with its memorable sign, *Preserving the heritage of death care*. The signage was chunky and set up on a pole high like at a motel. It had become one of the points on my world map, intricate details which signified I had my bearings. Soon there would be a sign for Bed, Bath and Beyond, which marked the comforting turn off for the Marriot.

In the hotel lobby, I hung back from reception and braced myself to move as fast as I could when called for my key. If I got caught, I might be persuaded to join the crew later in the bar and the pattern would continue to hold.

Behind the receptionist there was an oversized painting of a dandelion, which was supposed to support an air of breeziness as we went about our hotel existence. The carpet was modern, orange with claret flecks, possibly another flower design, but not so dissimilar to how red wine splatters when dropped. Most crew were off to shop at Greenspoint Mall, or 'gunspoint' as they phrased it with a special seasoning of cynicism and racism. Then they would meet for Happy Hour which began at five and went on until whenever. Some of the stewardesses had caught wind of a sale at the GAP outlet, and the captain and first officer were looking for recruits to go to the Houston Space Center.

I had my own mission, so once the key was in my hand I darted to the lift and pressed the button to close the door before anyone could come in. In my room I opened the jaw of my suitcase and took out the tub of green detox powder. Then I undid my skirt and rolled down my tights, letting my stomach breathe over the top of my knickers. Today my hips had knocked against several passengers' shoulders when I walked down the economy aisle. My thighs – I'd seen them in a photo Sharon had taken of me posing by an alcove on a beach in Bermuda. At the beginning of the year I'd taped the photo inside my notebook as a reminder of what I didn't want to look like. Last month I'd been to the uniform stores to swap my skirts for a size up. A few months before that, I found out that Sharon and her ex-girlfriend *had* had sex, but I still hadn't got to the bottom of where they'd done it. I'd sensed distance from Sharon for a while, a distraction, something like electrical interference, and I wondered if my constant accusations of her having sex with her ex had forced her into it.

It'd become clear one night in London when the ex-girlfriend had 'bumped into' us. She'd made an exaggerated point of inspecting me up and down, then overtly laughed about my weight to her friend. She was sporty, slim, blonde and I guessed based success on being all of these things. It was perhaps the cruellest thing one woman could do to another, to laugh at their body, which proved there was no such thing as female solidarity in the lesbian world. Sharon had made an obvious mistake of saying she hadn't noticed.

Remembering the betrayal all over again, how Sharon wouldn't tell me whose flat or whose bed, how many times, orgasms or not – it came at me like a knife. It broke my heart. Just when I thought I was done with the betrayal, I slumped, winded once again. The infidelity seemed to wait for these solitary moments when far from home. Leaning across to the bedside table, I picked up the pen from the notepad. Trying out its flow, I practised my signature a few times. The ink had the natural ease I liked. Then I got up, found the second pen by the room service menu and slotted them in my handbag. Propping up the room service menu on the pillow for my return later, I already knew what I would have – quesadilla with extra guacamole and sour cream, but still I knew it was important to give myself room to change my mind. Perhaps have a Caesar salad.

From my handbag, I pulled out the notebook and flipped it open. The page opposite the Bermuda thighs photo was full of drunken scrawl, something about Sharon and how she loved dogs. Flicking to a blank page, I wrote down: *The term 'air rage' enters the Collins dictionary for the first time.* I'd read it in the *Daily Mail* on the flight over and it'd struck me as an important turning point. How violence was now a common part of my job. These days the *Daily Mail* was the only choice of newspaper on board, which proved we were now in the conservative days of flying: no more *Guardian* or publications with a liberal bias. Even the *OK!* magazine had been axed to save money. And there were no more landing drinks, or 'bus juice' after each flight. Even Steve said he was no longer taking miniatures off the plane without paying for them. Along with the introduction of 100ml containers in everyone's hand luggage, crew surveillance was rumoured to be everywhere. Only last week a stewardess had been suspended for taking home two cold sausages from the first class oven for her cats. Now we had to make sure we had a receipt for everything. Not that I was drinking; I hadn't for six and a half days since the night out with Steve where I'd missed the kerb and fallen into the road. The bruise was only just leaving my arm, and the A&E nurse said the stitches would fall out of my hair by themselves.

I was free from the shame now I was incognito in Houston. I showered, dressed, packed my rucksack then quickly left the room. As I strode along the corridor, desperate to be outside in the open air, I heard the click of a hotel door and ran, pressing the lift button with a stabbing motion. Once the doors were closed behind me, I hid from my reflection and instead concentrated on the poster for the Friday Night Chinese Banquet. Its pile of spring rolls and glossy plum dipping sauce made me wish it wasn't a Tuesday.

The receptionist directed me to the nearest bus stop, which was a fifteen-minute walk out of the business park and along a street running parallel to the freeway. There was nothing else in walking distance, unlike other destinations such as Hong Kong with its parks and local shops: this was America, cars and freeways – even finding a bus stop was an endeavour in itself.

Soon I discovered a shelter, which I hoped was the stop. And when the bus drew up, I smiled and took the steps and greeted the driver, holding out dollar notes towards him.

'What was that?'

'I said hello,' I said, emphasising my British accent, as if it would protect me. 'Central Houston,' I added, and he beckoned me on, taking the dollars, with no ticket rolling out of his machine.

The bus was nearly full. Above the seats was the sign: NO GUNS, which was shocking. Everyone stared at me as if I were lost, so I sat next to an old woman with a pulled-down beanie, wisps of frizzy grey hair poking out. I smiled at her, and she bunched her arms up over her bosoms. As the bus pulled out onto the road, no one spoke. Everyone seemed exhausted. A man in sweatpants glanced over, keeping his eyes fixed on me as if it was a game of who would stop looking first. I was the tourist, so I studied the floor. Perhaps he was on his way back from work. It was one in the afternoon. I wanted to tell him how I too had just finished work. Find some common ground between us.

The old woman shifted her hip against me, but it wasn't until she started to stand that I understood she wanted to get off. There was no exchange, and I thought the woman must distrust me. Or was this the usual cocktail of post-flight paranoia and exhaustion kicking in? After the woman had gone I shifted into the window seat and imagined vodka pouring over ice. The cubes, stuck together so seamlessly at first, would find their fault-lines, and drop their shoulders. I would swirl the glass, tinkling the thickening liquid and sip it down, the funny hopeful girl coming back, cool burn calming, turning the key in the lock.

I cracked open my water bottle. Such a thirst. Six and a half days, nearly seven if I used UK time. The poet Emily Dickinson once wrote, 'thirst is understood by water.' However much I drank there was never enough understanding. The man in the sweatpants had now closed his eyes. I stared out of the misty window as the bus sped along, road after road, and wondered how I would know when we'd reached the centre of Houston. I should've asked the driver to do a shout out. I knew there was no river running through the city like the Hudson or Chicago River – this was oil country. I would wait until I could pluck up the courage to walk to the front of the bus. Then I decided, of course I would know when I found the centre, because as in New York or Chicago there would be shops and monuments. Soon the endless freeway would be interrupted with some kind of town planning, like widened pavements where people might be encouraged to walk. But, as the bus went on, stopping randomly here and there at pavements, endless stop signs, I realised how easy it would be to disappear and never find my way back. Lately I'd felt this desire to vanish, for my time not to be portioned up by the airline. All it would take was a sequence of buses, I could just go.

When the bus crossed a bridge, a line of skyscrapers appeared. Eventually I approached the driver, the concentration of tall buildings giving me a burst of optimism.

'Excuse me. I'd like to go to the Rothko Chapel please.'

'Where?'

'Rothko, the painter's chapel.'

'Sorry miss, I've not heard of the place.'

'Or perhaps the museum of fine art?'

'That'll be the museum district,' he said. 'About ten minutes.'

'Can you let me know?'

'Sure,' he said. 'Sure thing, ma'am.'

I sat back down, reassured by our conversation. Twenty minutes later, I realised the driver had forgotten. Or worse, not wanted to let me know. So I got out next to a grey industrial power plant and walked back along the closely mown grass by a throughfare. Over the way were a series of closed shops advertising PSYCHIC READINGS or NAILS. The sun beat down, hot and airless, and my water bottle was empty. I waited by the roadside watching the cars pass by, wondering what they thought of me, a woman on the road with no sign like Cindy Sherman in her famous black and white film still shot. I froze, like a mannequin, like I was an interesting two-dimensional version of myself. Then a vision appeared – a glinting yellow taxi. I flung out my arm, waving, smiling. Almost leaping.

'Rothko Chapel please,' I said, bending to the car window.

'Sure,' the driver said.

The back seat was taped together, and foam poked out of a hole. As we drove, I couldn't stop my finger slotting in and out, then I wound down the window. I caught the driver glancing into his mirror.

'Where you from?' the driver asked.

'London.'

'Wow. Ing-er-land. What you doing here?'

'I'm a journalist,' I said. Until that moment I hadn't considered being this, but now I had, it seemed obvious. Of course, I might be one. My own type of special reporter.

'I'm researching.'

'Researching Houston? I know a thing or two about this place. I moved here, well, twenty years back. And my, have we some ghosts.'

'Love,' I said. 'I'm looking into love and how different it might be, out here.'

'Ha, what I don't know about love,' he said. 'God is everywhere.' He splayed his hand towards the sky. 'Except the Muslims. You know? What they did . . .'

I wrote down 'God is everywhere' and looked out of the window, hoping he wouldn't expand on his Muslim comment. He thought it would be safe for him to say this because of how I looked. From crew I'd heard enough negative lazy generalisations to last me a lifetime. It didn't seem like the 'war on terror' was the only battle we had on our hands; what to do with all the violence, the anger shooting out, like weeds taking over derelict buildings? Hate never ended, it was always there in one form or other.

'I'm not into that,' I said, quietly, knowing this would be what a journalist would say.

'What's that?'

'Talking about Muslims. People are humans,' I said, growing into the journalist's voice.

'Oh, sure, sure. You know, I believe love is the same the world over,' he said. 'Mostly apart from ... Well, you're an intelligent woman. But God, well, he'll let you know if you're on the wrong path. Always does. Some disease'll get you, eventually, you know, if you're on the wrong path.'

This cab was a cage, I realised, and I was paying to be in it.

'You got a husband?'

'No,' I said, plucking foam out of the hole in the back seat. 'There was someone. But they're now ...I'm a widow.'

The cab driver said he was sorry. I felt the flip in the stomach of making up a story, of being able to play with the situation. It was the only way of protecting myself, to create a narrative he couldn't control, and which would also level his anger.

'I feel bad for you, being so young and alone,' he went on.

'But I am tall,' I said, not so quietly.

'Tall, eh? You'll be fine. What with your job and education. Some guy will be along soon to scoop you up. Or maybe not?' he said. 'Take my sister. She went to college, still isn't married. Said she wasn't interested in men, though I know she'll meet the right one soon. It's God's way. Creation. The next generation. You know.'

I slunk down in my seat, closing my eyes, then pressed

my fingers in my ears and listened to the compacted noise. The fare increased, digit by digit. We didn't seem to be getting anywhere. Perspiration built up round my neck like a collar. The driver could be taking me for a ride. His voice, I wanted to keep it shut out of me. I brushed the skin of my arm to remind myself of where I began, and where the cab ended. The meter was on twenty-four dollars. When I glanced again it was thirty-two.

At forty-two dollars the cab finally slowed, turning into a long suburban street with patchwork lawns and skinny driveways. The chapel was on the left behind a rectangle of water as green as wine-bottle glass. The edge of the pond was so precise, it was as if it'd been punched in the ground.

Passing through the entrance I stepped into a spacious octagonal room. On the ground, three bald-headed figures sat cross-legged in orange robes. Red and purple floor-to-ceiling paintings hung on every wall. It was about ten degrees cooler, and I rubbed my arms to stop goosebumps. Then I sat upright on one of the benches, lined up like pews. Automatically, I clasped my hands together and my head dropped.

The absence of noise was full and intense. I was used to the constant womb-like muffle of air conditioning on the aircraft, so much so only now did I realise it was missing. As I studied the room, I opened my eyes as wide as I could, hoping Rothko's paintings would provide an answer. Once when I was an art student visiting The National Gallery, I'd seen a Rothko painting pulse in the centre of the canvas. Apparently, Dali used to force his eyes to be as open as possible so he could absorb the whole world all at once.

I rested, taking in a particular painting which spoke to me. I stared and stared and let myself relax. Here I was, I thought. Left to be free from expectation. The world had texture. No one would ever find me here in a spiritual art gallery, with real monks sat meditating on the floor with their legs crossed. No one would be able to take me away.

After a while, it began. Like a frog's heart visible through its neck, a beat appeared in the painting. This was when I started to cry. Not the kind of tears which rose up and caught your throat in dramatic sobs, the water just plopped down my face, rising and streaming out through my eyes and onto the back of my hand.

I rubbed my nose, then took out my notebook and wrote, *I think*. Then I looked about, waiting for something more to come. There must be a formula in these situations – I once used to be able to express myself without worrying. Jumped into notions and play. I let my mind go blank, which in turn created more blankness the consistency of thick white bread. I worried how these days it was all too easy to be empty.

I hate Sharon, I wrote. *And her anorexic desires and the way she once called me 'sugar-tits'.* A tear spilled onto the notebook into the ink, swelling the unrefined words. *She cheated on me, even though she pretended she didn't. With a woman who is thin, shiny, hairless downstairs. A woman who looks like a heterosexual woman trying to please men, but then just shags Sharon. She thinks she's got it all, but all she has is looks.* I kept writing in an attempt to purge the pain. Soon there were no new ideas about Sharon, so I began to write about home and the L Gang and needing to find a way out of the airline. But so many crew were saying the same thing, and no one knew how to go about finding another job.

A white bird appeared next to me on the bench. When I glanced up it was a hand sliding a tissue in my direction. A plump woman with tight brown curls, wearing a flowery blouse, bent towards me. Her breasts were weighing over her waistband and I really wanted to touch them.

'There,' she said. 'We have the hankies here. Everyone that arrives is welcome.'

'Thank you,' I mouthed, noticing the lines of her elbow creases.

'You've come a very long way to be here,' she said. And I nodded, sensing she didn't mean air miles.

'I have,' I said, and a prayer bell tinged, and it was a pure round sound.

Though the sky had darkened early to indigo, the Texan air was still warm. During my search for a return bus stop I discovered a Kroger supermarket and bought a pack of sushi with a fish-shaped bottle of soy sauce. Sitting on the kerb in the car park, I practised using chopsticks on the Californian rolls. Facing a row of closed shop units, I cast my eye over the dresses in Winnie's Couture Bridal Fashion, noting how sinister and out of date they all were.

By the time I found my way back to the hotel, the crew were bedded in for Happy Hour. Giant navy paper shopping bags sat around the stewardess' feet while the captain and first officer stood together in their matching customary Chinos. Baseball played on screens, and I wished I could slope in for some free chicken wings from the silver trough. Instead I jumped in the elevator, leaving the ground before anyone saw me.

Safely back in my room, I pulled out the wine I'd purchased at Kroger. I'd had a conversation with the shop assistant about a dinner party and how I'd been asked to get two bottles. I'd told her we were having fish, cod, and she'd suggested two whites totalling over forty dollars. From the bar area in my room, I grabbed the ice box and went along the corridor, strolling, my outside eye positioned on myself, watching how I wasn't rushing. There was no desperation here, proving I wasn't an alcoholic. When I pressed the button of the ice machine, it spat out cubes, pausing between each release, as if deciding how much to give me.

Back on the sofa, I studied the label on the bottles: *14 percent, Contains Sulphites*. Tapping the glass, I knew I didn't have to drink it. I could pad dirty underwear round the bottles in my suitcase and take them home for when I'd achieved a bigger milestone of not drinking, like three weeks. How hard would it be to go without it for a month? But how boring would it be? And who would I hang out with? Mum was the only person I knew who didn't drink.

Reception ordered me the taxi for the lesbian bar, Sue Ellen's. They said twenty minutes, so I put on mascara, aware of the unopened bottles on the side, staring them down, shaking my head at them, thinking how I'd promised. Surely, I'd done this once before in adult life without even thinking about it? The Rothko Chapel had woken me up after a long dream. Something true had chimed when I had written in the notebook. When I left, I'd gone outside and noticed the exact outline of the trees. There had been abnormally loud birdsong. I'd smiled at a man washing his car and it had all been light and easy.

The taxi ride to the bar was good and silent. When I got there, I would go straight to the bar and order Diet Coke with ice and a lemon slice to make it more of a drink. Just an hour, then I'd come back and rent an in-house movie as a reward.

The driver stopped outside a bar with blackened windows

and a flashing neon Budweiser sign. Next door was JR's, the gay men's bar, which seemed busier. I was dressed in navy jeans with turn ups, a Breton striped top and Converse trainers, which was my favourite outfit. My hair was cut shorter than usual, so I had lost most of my femininity. I hoped there would be line dancing and at least one attractive single woman. When the bouncer asked for my ID, I showed him my passport and he ushered me in.

The air conditioning was on full, so I would have to keep moving. There was a sunken dance floor to the left, and empty tables on a raised level to the side.

'Hi. What can I get you?' the bartender asked.

'Diet Coke,' I said, like clockwork, I could do this; easy-peasy. But as I stood there the sentence began to beg for a different ending.

'Is that all ma'am?'

Why couldn't she just start making the drink? My hand went to my back pocket to search for my notepad. It wasn't there, just my room card and passport. I'd left it by the bedside.

'No,' I said, examining the twinkling bottles behind her on the shelf. 'Diet Coke, and . . .a vodka.'

'Single or double? It's Happy Hour – buy one get one free.'

'Single,' I said, decisively.

Maybe I could ask for the first one now, and get the second drink later?

'No, hold on . . .you know what?' I said, letting out a little laugh, as if realising my mistake.

'Make it a double. Thanks.'

Two drinks arrived, double doubles, each with buoyant black straws.

I sipped the first, telling myself to make it last half an hour. The cola tasted metallic, out of a pipe. A woman in a leather vest moved slowly around the tables with tequila bottles belted to her hips. On the dance floor a few women in checked shirts and cowboy boots stepped from side to side. When a Dolly Parton song came on, the dancers swung into couples and it all seemed hopeless. There were not enough lesbians to go round. It was then that I noticed a wide-bottomed woman come to the bar with her thumb slotted into another woman's back-pocket. A third soon stood beside them chatting. Her hair was divided into plaits, and she wore tight jeans which cupped her bottom cheeks.

I finished my second drink and decided to ask an old companion to join me, white wine. I returned to the bar with the empty glasses. Servers liked this, I knew.

'A large glass of Chardonnay,' I said, leaning on an elbow.

Upon hearing my accent, the woman with the plaits turned. By the way she nearly smiled, I could tell she might be interested. We got talking, chit chat about the temperature of the bar. The wine emboldened me, made me interesting.

'I'm from a gay magazine in London. Would you mind if I asked you a few questions?'

'London,' the woman said. 'Sure.'

Her name was Kelsey. She drove a Mustang. When she said she didn't touch alcohol, it rang alarm bells, but it turned out she had a brother who was a recovering alcoholic in rehab. She'd grown up outside of Houston in a place called Marble Falls where her mother trained horses, and now had opened a holistic training centre where people could be with the animals. She managed a pet store in a shopping mall while she figured out what was her next step. There was something unsophisticated about her, but because she believed I was a writer, I began to relax, and the horse therapy was interesting. She was a deep thinker. Love was different depending on who you were with, time specific and yet universal. She told me when a horse smelt human pain they would run in circles until all their adrenaline was emptied out.

It was gone ten by the time we arrived at the hotel. Three in the morning London time, by rights I should've been exhausted. I'd learnt as long as I kept a certain level of alcohol pumping round my system, I could dodge jet lag and then binge sleep for twelve to fourteen hours until normal again.

While Kelsey parked the car, I made an excuse to go up to the bedroom. Pulling the airline shirt and skirt off the hangers, I threw it all in the suitcase. Mixing the three digits of the lock so she couldn't open the case, I noticed the ice had melted in the box. It would take less than a minute to fetch fresh to chill the wine behind the shower curtain before she knocked on the door. So I retrieved more ice, crunched in the bottle, then opened it. I unpacked my wash bag, the tiny mouth freshener the good quality one from Denver. I smoothed the bed, then stood back, seeing the room through the eyes of a Texan woman who might soon kiss a British journalist. The number of pillows, eight counting the stupid ones, took on a sudden splendour.

After downing a beaker of wine, I swilled my mouth with the minty wash. Gay men knew what to do in these situations. Steve had once had a liaison with a stranger in a sauna. He'd asked why there weren't lesbian saunas and I'd explained having outside genitals made things more accessible, less fiddly than when they were folded away.

I kissed my forearm, little pecks, pretending my lips were Kelsey's. I could sense her arrival and so I swigged another glass to find the lift off. I reapplied mascara in the bathroom, thinking she would knock any minute now. God, I was beautiful in the mirror. My reflection was lovely. Look at her eyes, I thought. Green as olives. She was more like the person I was supposed to be.

Sitting on the bed, I swung my feet, while waiting for Kelsey's knock at the door. I hadn't thought of Sharon all evening. Now I had, I punched a pillow, then brought it back to life by whacking the sides together. Sharon's body came to mind. Probably the finest, so I punched the pillow again. Then I remembered the chambermaid and put the pillows right.

The wait for Kelsey had gone on too long. My energy was beginning to dip; maybe she'd gone home. I couldn't tell whether it had been mere minutes or half an hour, so I went down, through reception and into the car park. Circling round pickup trucks and motorbikes, I plucked a leaf from the bush and snapped it, saying the word 'photosynthesis', proving I still knew it from school. Not many people used the word. I wondered how many cabin crew still knew the word.

A blue reflection wavered up the side of the hotel. I found a clearing in the hedge then saw the kidney-shaped pool floodlit by underwater lights. Opening the gate, I went to the water's edge and sat on the warm concrete. Flipping off my shoes, I rolled up my jeans and dangled my feet in the water. There was a flap you could swim through which went to an inner hotel pool. The lights were on in the gym, a man's head bobbing up and down on a treadmill.

'There you are.'

I turned. Kelsey was at the gate, her face lit by the pool. In this light her forehead seemed bulbous, as if she had a growth, or a moon pressing from behind the skin.

'I thought you'd disappeared on me.'

A breeze picked up. I could feel the warmth of Kelsey's thigh as she sat down beside me. She took off her trainers and socks, then rolled up her jeans. In the trick of water, I watched her feet become foreshortened. I remembered the wine upstairs, which made me feel enthusiastic for the night ahead. Journalists had deadlines. There was an end to their work.

'I had a wander about,' Kelsey said. 'This hotel's so cool. I would've never known it was here.'

'It's okay,' I said. 'I prefer the Renaissance group. Dressing gowns. With the little soaps, you know.'

Kelsey had nothing to add. Of course she didn't. She probably hadn't set foot outside of Houston. Why would she, when the size of Texas was bigger than the whole of the United Kingdom? With that the pool gate creaked open and two women came in carrying cocktails. They dragged metal chairs over to a table, making a noise on the cement. Then they lit cigarettes and flicked back their heads, exhaling smoke. They began to stare over. Then one of them give a little wave.

'Do you know them?' Kelsey whispered.

'No, is it you they're signalling at?' I said.

After searching through my mind, I realised they were two stewardesses from my crew.

'Oh,' I said. 'They must have me confused with someone else.'

The two women kept checking over. I could see they were talking about us.

'My research shows gay women in London are body fassists,' I said.

'Oh?' Kelsey said.

'Sorry, fassists,' I repeated. My mind felt sharp, but my words wouldn't find their shape.

'Body fascists,' Kelsey said, softly.

'Yes, that's right,' I said. 'Is it the same here then?'

'Kind of,' Kelsey said, staring at the mosaic on the base of the pool. I tried to work out what the pattern was. A swan, or the M from Marriot?

'Is that a fish?' I said.

'What?' Kelsey said.

'In the pool.' I pointed.

She glanced down, shook her head, then leant back examining the side of the hotel. I counted the rooms, realising mine was on the other side. Knowing I might be reading her thoughts, how she must be thinking about sex, I wasn't sure I wanted to take her up to my room now.

'So, what are you going to write about Houston?' she asked.

There was no moon. I knew there were stars behind the clouds, but I couldn't see them.

'I'll come up with an ankle,' I said. 'Angle.'

'What will you call it? The story?'

I thought about it. '"Happy Hour", probably,' I said, letting out a little laugh.

'You know, I read this short story called that once,' she said. 'It included this part how, in ancient Europe "happy hour" was the moment between dog and wolf, where outside a walled city, Italy probably, a canine paced about in the shadows, and it couldn't be distinguished as friend or enemy – you know. Like the effects of alcohol. I've always remembered that.'

'I did not know that,' I said. 'Who wrote it?'

'Some American woman writer. I majored in English. Wrote half a novel once.'

'You wrote half a novel?' I said. 'What happened to it?'

'Nothing,' she said. 'Nothing happened to it. I got so far and hit a wall. I'm the one working at a pet store, remember? You're lucky to work with words for money. I admire that.'

I had not remembered the pet store until now. I wished she hadn't reminded me of all the cages and hamster wheels; her fallen ambition felt like creeping mould.

Up the side of the hotel, I studied the windows and saw the curtains lit by the rooms behind. There was so much potential in those little boxes. Someone could be writing, writing like a proper author, only stopping to answer the door for room service. Writers lived in hotels across Europe. Every hotel room had a desk with more than one pen. It was as if they were instructing us all to begin. Get it all down. Go mad, then shoot your wife in the head with a bow and arrow.

I checked over at the stewardesses. One of them had gone inside. I hadn't noticed her leave. Even though there was clearly an empty chair, in my mind they'd both been there, sat like sentinels at the gate to my freedom. Clearly, I was able to leave with Kelsey at any point, but when I closed my eyes, there was something bigger than me pressing me to the concrete, making circles with my feet in the water, forcing my hands to grip the edge of the pool.

I was sure I had only gone for a moment, but when I

opened my eyes, it was because I heard Kelsey. She was getting up, brushing the backs of her jeans.

'Are you going?' I said.

'Yep, I don't think you're really up for this,' she said. 'Maybe get some sleep, you know?' And I presumed she might offer to help pull me up, but instead she headed for the gate and, stopping momentarily to lift her hand, let it swing shut behind her.

CHAPTER 7

The Summer, Before The Dark

LHR – LAX – LHR

This was LAX, the land of the third-act twist where relationships had back-stories, omelettes had stations and deer drank from swimming pools. We were sunbathing on Steve's hotel room terrace, and I was trying to discuss the light. How it was the result of air trapped between ocean, mountains, and desert. I had carried the Lonely Planet USA over in my bag to spend time searching for specifics to tighten my brain. On the flight I'd met Uri Geller, who had bent a spoon in front of the crew in the business class galley. After I'd joked I could feel my bra wire twisting, but it all got a bit lost in the moment.

'To think we get paid for this,' Steve said. Lifting his drink, the sun curved in the straw-coloured bowl.

'I know,' I said, plopping ice into my glass. 'Paid to drink wine. Paid to stay drunk. Shouldn't we plan something, for later?'

'Need to relax me tootsies first,' he said, glancing over a bit puzzled. 'Did you know if you massage your big toe, it helps headaches?'

'Is that so,' I said. 'So if you massage your head, will it help your toe?' We'd been drinking since we arrived. Unbeknown to Steve, I'd managed to cut back a little on my days off and have one night alcohol-free. But I didn't tell him this because I was worried who we'd be with one another if we didn't consume alcohol.

Earlier this morning in London, I'd locked my front door, but when I pushed against it, although it didn't move against my shoulder, it still hadn't felt locked. All the way to the train station it was like I'd forgotten something, and I had checked my keys, work pass, passport, on-board gilet etc. – all of which were there. In the end I'd rung Mum from the airport to ask her to see if I'd left the iron on. She'd come back with a negative. She sounded flat, because of Dad.

'Mum told me this morning, the other week she'd said to Dad, "It's me or the drink."'

'Really? I didn't know things were that bad. What did he say?' Steve asked.

I pondered for a while because I felt embarrassed for what I was about to divulge.

'He pleaded with Mum to stay. He was on his knees, begging her. It's so sad.'

'So, what happened next?'

'He said, he didn't want to live without drink, or Mum.'

'I couldn't imagine thinking like that,' he said. 'Not your lovely mum.'

'Me neither,' I said, knowing I could think exactly like that. Sometimes all I did think was when I could have a glass of something. Which social situation I could concoct so it would seem normal to open the bottle.

'Might as well get the other bottle out,' Steve said. 'And press play on the music while you're there.'

'Sure,' I said, acting relaxed about the wine. This was who we were together, this was what we did. There were no edges then. I fitted into him and him into me. It reminded me of being small with Mum, curved onto her lap, the dog on top, a mix of skin and fur and scent.

I padded over to the kitchenette. By some fluke Steve had been upgraded to a suite with two electric hob rings and a mock-wood kitchenette. The corner sofa was partitioned from the bed by glass-bricks and through sliding doors was a wide terrace overlooking Ruby's Diner. When the traffic went quiet, we could hear the boats in the harbour chinking, the metal ropes tapping their masts in the wind.

I pressed play on the CD player, then forwarded it to the duet between George Michael and Elton John. Opening the fridge, I took out the overpriced olives and fresh bottle of Chardonnay. Earlier, as soon as our suitcases had been delivered, we'd changed out of our uniforms, showered, then headed up to Whole Foods, the Californian phenomenon. We'd never seen a supermarket like it, and I had prided myself on visiting a supermarket in every location I went – in a life of hotel rooms, these were one of the few places where I felt I was someplace real. But Whole Foods was like an art gallery with its displays of bulbous organic lemons and piles of vacuum-packed blue corn tortillas. I'd gazed at the huge prawns in the chiller, dreaming of being invited to an American barbeque, then spent time grinding fresh coffee beans in a machine to take back home, careful not to spend too much money. There were seven types of lettuce kept wet by a timer-operated mist. Steve and I had waited, putting out our hands into the cool cascade of vapour.

We'd bought two nine-dollar bottles – a sensible amount to get going – and a tub of olives, some smoked cheese and sliced ham. Like all cabin crew currently we were on the Atkins diet, which consisted of eating only protein. You weren't supposed to drink alcohol, but you could lose weight without exercising. Apart from bad breath and constipation, there seemed very little wrong with the diet, although Dr Atkins was rumoured to have died of pulmonary heart failure.

'Wait,' Steve said, lifting his finger. When the line in the song arrived about searching himself, and seeing someone else, he sang it out loud with feeling. He got up, retrieved his zip-folder of CDs then began flipping through the frosted pouches. I offered him an olive and he put one in his mouth, scraping the flesh from the stone with a side tooth. I re-registered his beauty, then I pushed my weight back in my chair, tugged down my swimsuit, and placed an ankle on one knee so the sun hit my inner thigh.

It often took a while for the two litres of water drunk on the aircraft to travel up from my swollen ankles to my bladder. Closing the door to Steve's bathroom, I saw my chest was burnt, so I helped myself to some factor 30 and then squirted on some aftershave. My hair was now cut short. At thirty-one, the strands had turned from golden blonde to the colour of dark wheat, as if I was in a season on the turn.

The bottle in the fridge was a screw top, like the miniatures on board. Going back into the sun, I set it on the patio table. Over the road, a dog walker wearing a fuchsia pink sun-visor turned the corner onto the sidewalk.

'There's your girlfriend,' Steve said.

'Huh,' I said, not finding it funny. We counted one Shih Tzu, a Bulldog and the third we couldn't make out, but it had long tan ears and a diamante studded collar. Each dog panted in the heat, their leads stretching in front of the woman.

I topped up the wine, giving more to Steve to show how I didn't have an issue.

Across the way the dogs started to bark.

'Look at that dog walker's socks,' I said.

'What about them?' Steve said.

'They're so white, as if they never get dirty,' I said, trying to find a way in. I wanted to talk to Steve this trip, really talk. 'Do you ever, I mean, want to get under the surface ... To feel like you're more inside your life? We never really get to find out what's going on wherever we go. Dipping in and out all the time. And the airline, they pay us to not feel real.'

'Do you feel unreal then?'

'Yes,' I said, relieved that he might know what I meant. 'Sometimes I just see someone and think, what's inside their fridge?'

'You want to know what people in Los Angeles keep inside their fridge?'

'You know what I mean.'

He studied me for a moment. 'You know I once went back to this guy's house in Atlanta. He had a chest freezer full of horse meat.'

'You're kidding.'

'I left quickly. Bad karma. So you want to get deeper, I get that.'

'You do?' I said.

'Of course,' he said.

'Well then, if only we could get invited round someone's

house, we might start to make some connections. But it takes ages to get to know people before they'll ask you back.'

'The only way to get invited in by a stranger is for a one-night stand,' Steve said. 'And there's just the one gay bar round here, unless we go to West Hollywood.'

'But it's not about sex,' I said. 'Locals chat nice enough to us in the supermarket – the guy who packed our bags earlier for instance, all he wanted to do was tell me he was quarter-Scottish – but that's as far as it goes. I bet they'd open up if there was an emergency.'

'Like an earthquake?'

'They do have them here, but I don't think it's wise to wish for one.'

We watched the walker pause by Dive 'n' Surf to take a phone call. Then she followed the path in the direction of the beach. The dogs pulled, knowing the routine. I thought about their owners. Each with their jobs, with particular reasons for not being able to walk their dog regularly.

'Dogs,' I exclaimed, loudly.

Steve turned and frowned. 'What about them?'

'They have stories attached to them. Human lives.'

The afternoon light seemed more focused now, out of its haze, so we began to hatch a plan. To make it convincing, I explained how we would need a prop, costumes, but we only had what was in our suitcases and a couple of duty free carrier bags. By the time the empty vodka miniatures were placed in the bin, we'd decided on a story. Our precious dog, an eight-year-old Dalmatian named Dolly, which we'd flown all the way from England at great expense, had gone missing.

We left the Crowne Plaza, feeling conspicuous in the

bright sun, passing The Salvation Army building onto North Harbour Drive. As we wandered along, I kept walking into Steve, as if he were a magnet, so I moved purposefully near the kerb, trying to stay in a straight line.

As we passed the imitation Spanish missions we held hands. I could feel his knuckle under my thumb. We both knew we could easily pass as husband and wife because sometimes people asked if we were married. In photographs we mirrored each other's body language, and this could be misinterpreted by the uninitiated, or those who walk about never considering the world might not be as straight as they think.

Last Christmas in Harare, we'd tried having sex with each other, but it hadn't worked. We didn't really like to talk about it now, how I'm sure neither of us had been surprised – it had been brewing. I had suspected (and feared) for a while that if the moment came, we might forget our homosexual natures. I remembered that night, how after we had got on the bed we had kissed, and our teeth had knocked together. Then I'd told him he should kiss me more softly, not like he would a man. Fuller lips. Not biting and probing with his tongue. 'Kiss me like I'm a woman, and you're a woman,' I remember saying. When he'd tried what he thought this was, it was still too forceful. When I opened my eyes, I couldn't ignore how his penis, which had momentarily been as hard as a dog chew, had relaxed. It seemed so sad to me, how we were both so attracted to one another, but not in a way which translated into what we could understand.

'The movie house,' I said. 'There's the dream house I told you about.' I slipped my fingers from his, flexing out the damp and we stood admiring the bougainvillea. Then he walked backwards to take a photo of the white-washed low-rise with the Mexican tiled archway, the garden full of palms and round squat succulents.

'Remember your face wouldn't be calm. You've lost our dog,' I reminded him. 'Say out loud *my dog has gone* and work out how you would feel, if it were true.'

'My dog has disappeared. We were out together,' Steve rehearsed, trying to dig into real sentiment. 'She slipped the lead when she saw a squirrel, and then whoosh.'

'They don't have squirrels here.'

'No?' he said.

'They have coyotes and wild pigs.'

'Right. So, where do we live then? Obviously, our accents are a giveaway,' Steve said.

'We're staying at the hotel. With work.'

'Which job?'

'I'm writing a screenplay,' I said, thinking how I could write a screenplay. I could go to the library and get a book out on it. It seemed so obvious now. Or a novel, I could write half a novel first, then the other half next.

'What if they ask about the film?'

'They won't ask. This is L.A. Everyone's writing a film. No one's interested really. But, if they do ask, act like you've had a breakdown. That's what's slowing down my writing career. Looking after you. My sick husband.'

'I wouldn't have a breakdown. I'm not like that.' Steve looked annoyed and did the tense shoulder thing. I could smell his boozy breath, so I checked my pockets for gum, because mine must be the same, but there wasn't any. 'This is a crazy idea.'

'This is it here,' I said, stopping at the apartment block. Metal letters attached to the front wall spelt out *La Catalina*.

'The Catherine,' translated Steve, and I loved that he knew a bit of Spanish. We passed through the arch surrounded by orange beaked flowers and into a square courtyard with a trickling fountain. In the far corner was a front door, propped open by a trainer. A lengthy cactus stood in a blue glazed pot. I nodded towards it and as we approached, we heard a crowd cheer on a TV.

There was an attractive white buzzer set amidst deep blue Mexican tiles. I pressed it and we waited until a shadow walked to the screen door, a topless man in low sweatpants.

'Excuse me,' I said, through the screen. 'Sorry to disturb you. But I don't suppose you've seen a dog run by?' As I spoke, I could hear how English and how fake this sounded.

'Huh?' He pushed open the door then flicked his cigarette to the side, brushing his hand over a line of dark hair which ran to his stomach. Steve's eyes were all over it.

'We lost her. We were walking by the condos, and she ran off. So sorry, we don't know the area. Just checked into the Crowne Plaza. We're here for business.'

'Oh man, that's bad. What breed?'

'Dalmatian. She slipped her lead,' I said, lifting the duty free carrier bag as if it contained something of the dog.

'I haven't seen anything round here. We're enclosed, you know?'

'Oh. Could we check out the back? I mean, do you have a garden?'

'She means the yard,' Steve said.

I threw him a side-look.

'The only access to the back is from a locked gate, but there's a low fence so, I suppose, in reality a dog could get in. I'll go and check for sure. What's its name?'

'Dolly,' I said.

Our plan was working, he'd believed us. This was enough, but then Steve's mouth twitched, and my mouth jerked, so I pressed the smile from it. Then I noticed a leg over the arm of the couch, in front of the TV. Not a movie star kind of leg. A thick female ankle. As I moved forward to get a better look, I smelt stale cigarette smoke in the gauze of the screen and as the man opened his back door, I noticed him tucking something in the back of his pants.

'Did you see that?' I mouthed, indicating towards the back of my shorts.

'Yes,' Steve whispered. 'Has he got a gun?'

'Maybe,' I replied. Then I thought how he could and made a gesture with my thumb to go. Steve shook his head.

'Let's see what happens,' he whispered.

'Like what? See if he finds our dog?'

'Ssssh. He might still invite us in. You know, for a beer.'

'His girlfriend's on the sofa. Don't be ridiculous.'

'It might be his sister. Besides, this is a game. To go deeper, remember?'

When the man came back, he shook his head.

I felt disappointed. It was hard to disbelieve that there wasn't something of ours out there now. Then out of the blue, Steve held out a piece of hotel note paper towards the man, as I tried to read what was on it.

'That's my room number ... So, if you find Dolly, just call me.'

The guy stared at Steve, then at me. He studied the note, brushed his nose, then took it. I studied Steve's neck, the nerve of him.

'Sure,' the man said, and we quickly moved away, across the courtyard and through the iron gate, speed-walking along the road until we were far enough to let the laughter burst out.

There was a liquor store to the right of the parking lot. As we went towards it, the automatic doors opened emitting cool air conditioning. I took the aisle dedicated to jumbo packets of Lays.

Restocked, we headed for the beachfront houses overlooking Redondo beach. Painted in baby blues, creamy pinks and salmon hues, some were modernist structures with wide windows and spiral staircases leading up to roof gardens. Out front were dining spaces with tables, loungers and barbeques covered in plastic protectors. The beach was practically empty, and the houses all locked up. A few people played volleyball, while a group of teenage girls sat on a blanket. Gulls rested like pottery figures on the sand, their legs hidden under their chests. We headed towards a lifeguard tower and sat down, and I pushed my feet through the warm sand to find the cool underneath. Waves crashed into white foam, and we swigged beer from bottles in brown paper bags, checking over our shoulders for the police.

There were no swimmers, and soon the wet sand became silver. Moments later a light aircraft flew over in the sky with a sideways bottle of Malibu trailing behind, the lettering back to front. *The New Malibu Island Melon.* I watched the plane disappear remembering how, since childhood, I'd longed for a message in a bottle, but one washed up from the sea with a note rolled up in it. And now here one was: an advert for drink flying across the sky.

By six o'clock we'd finished the beers. As the sun dipped, the light in the east fell to blue, while the west sunk into orange. I rubbed my eyes awake. We had hours before bedtime, but without the sun the beach was losing its glory. Steve pulled me up and we took the wide stretch of sand back to the esplanade.

We moved along in a companionable silence. Steve a fraction in front, impatient for the night ahead, while I enjoyed the twilight. Joggers were out, and a skateboarder sped noisily by. It was then I noticed the familiar figure of a young girl up ahead, nine or ten years old, with blonde hair in bunches. As she got close, I registered her knock-knees and tanned calves. And when nearer still, how the right leg was covered with a square of gauze held by strips of medical tape. She was singing a song to herself, and I halted, letting Steve go on, knowing there was a presence about this girl. When she was about two metres away, I knew I shouldn't have been staring so hard, so like a pervert, because now I had broken her song, and her eyes met mine. Her expression was blank, waiting for me to speak, but I said nothing because I knew who she was.

In a photo album at home was a picture of myself on Brighton beach with my hair parted in the exact same way, a band either side making the bunches bouncy. On my right knee was a plaster where I'd fallen on the pebbles. I must have been nine or ten, wearing a little pink smock with a white lace trim around the neck. She was wearing a pink hoodie, little white shorts.

'Hello,' I said, softly, as she turned to look for someone. I knew what was coming next and lifted my hand to my nose and searched along the path. On cue a woman appeared, sunglasses, denim cut offs. Her mother.

'Can I help you?' she said. I knew she was going to reach swiftly for her daughter, then press her hand on her back, say 'come on darling' and move her along. I knew I would stay rooted to the spot and then say, 'no you're alright, I was just thinking about . . .' and then I would go quiet because I could not say, not outwardly, something which would make me sound insane, like 'I know this girl because she is me and there can be two of us and it's nothing to be scared of.' The déjà vu had taken hold and life taken on a texture of before, and again, and then all in the now. I waited for the scene to play itself out, waiting for the record to finish the track – I had no choice and didn't want a choice because being in this moment was fascinating and assuring. At art college I had experienced many an occasion where I knew what was coming, just before it had. On cue, Steve turned and waved at me to hurry up and I shouted, while knowing I was going to shout, 'I'm coming.'

'You okay?' Steve said, when I got to him. 'You're all pink.'

'Tired,' I said, the texture of the spell leaving me. 'That girl, she looked just like me. I mean, I think she was me, when I was younger.'

'You're all over the place,' he said, and slipped his arm into mine. 'You probably need some water.'

At the end of the boardwalk, I turned to check for the girl. Her mother was holding her hand. Even though it didn't make total sense, I knew we were meant to meet. When I got back to my hotel room, I would write it all down. It was important. The signs were coming for a reason. The first line would be: *The message is not in the bottle, it is in the girl.*

Hours later, the phone rang.

Here's a bed, I thought. *There's a mirrored wardrobe.* This was not my bed though. I recalled an argument. Accusing someone of stealing my jacket in a bar. I rolled over, found an empty vodka miniature digging into my breast from my bra. My purse was on the pillow, along with my airline pass. Zipped up, a hundred dollars folded inside. I hadn't spent any money. My passport was next to it. I lifted the receiver to make the phone stop ringing.

'Hello?'

Silence. I checked about the room. There was a travel kettle. The CD player and portable speakers. It was Steve's room. I felt sick. Swinging my legs to the floor, the bed lurched. I wanted water, so put my hand on the desk chair. The thatched black material vibrated a low-level pulse. I remembered my last trip, how the sofa had trembled in Arizona and the threesome with a pretty stewardess who wanted to impress her boyfriend.

The cover on the right-hand side of the bed was pulled back showing a crumpled sheet where Steve must've lain earlier. There was his light-weight jacket across the pillow.

'Steve? Are you here?'

I dropped back into the pillows on the bed. The aertex ceiling turned ninety degrees, then went round again, a double of it playing over the first image. My eyes kept trying to correct my vision. I gripped the seam of the mattress. We'd gone to a gay bar, I remembered now. He'd hooked up with the guy from *La Catalina*. Dropped me off in a car.

The clock radio said it was 00.11 which meant it was 8.11 a.m. in London. I felt as if I'd committed a crime, so I closed my eyes, but the bed moved again, this time spinning round, my stomach moving with it. Just keep breathing, I told myself. *Sleep will take you away, just hold on. Sleep will help you, the little cleaning army will appear.* I tried to imagine my inside team filling their tiny buckets, getting ready for the nightshift. But they were placing their mops to the side of the buckets. There was talk of a strike. An angry picket line. Airline unions were getting involved. So I began counting through the alphabet, an A – Z of all the countries I had been to: Australia, Barbados, Canada, Dad, Everywhere, Footstool . . .

CHAPTER 8

The Absence of Battery Life

LHR – HRE – LHR

I woke in the shade, swimsuit straps hanging off my shoulders. My sunbathing spot was set apart from the others. I was stationed in front of the closed beauty salon, where once stewardesses had enjoyed cheap pedicures. The cobalt water of the huge pool was a fraction away from my toes, so close I could be tipped in for a joke.

Earlier, after visiting the orphanage, I'd returned, positioning myself away from my crew who were lined up like smoking kippers. I couldn't get comfy as I had developed a shooting pain in my lower back. Since joining the airline, like many crew, I had been introduced to the children's orphanages when down route in the many African countries we visited. Specific relationships had been made with the orphanage in Nairobi where someone would deliver toys, clothes, medical supplies and donations. I was unaware if anyone had forged a relationship with the orphanages in Harare and since the sighting of the girl in LAX I had gone to an internet café to research girl's orphanages here, as I felt a great need to do something good, something worthwhile.

A lot of the crew couldn't bear it, and each time I visited I was reminded why. Today the orphan girls had sung for me, and then later I'd been shown the graves. But mostly these were happy places, full of learning and caring teachers. The children did not know any different and clearly they were like other kids, singing, playing, often laughing.

The late afternoon shadows from the trees had arrived and the crew had all moved inside, leaving towels bunched on the loungers. They'd been complaining that they couldn't believe the unions let us stay in this hotel, since the five-star standards had slipped.

Colder now, earlier it had been so hot I'd brazened the freezing pool. The only way was to jump in, and when I had, I felt my heart momentarily stop. For the first time I realised my heart was a machine, a piston with a pump in the cavity of my chest. As I recovered, flooding with oxygen, I remember saying to my body, *I will stop travelling in you like it's a free ride. I will learn to be inside of you all the time again.*

The trees were losing their leaves in the strong wind. There was a splash, and a set of shiny pink arms flapped in the deep end of the water. It was the captain's son, not at school, rising and falling, with his little fat boobs, gasping for air while performing a butterfly stroke towards his mother, the captain's wife. I couldn't work out how a pool could remain so chilled in the heat of Zimbabwe, as if by night the management floated ice in it. But they wouldn't be able to afford the ice now. Soon enough the boy doggie-paddled his way across and up the metal steps where the wife crouched with a towel. From here I tried to inspect the quality of the material, whether the hotel had given them preferential treatment, compared to the balding stock provided to us main crew.

Once there had been a dedicated pool boy who wore a white polo shirt and Bermuda shorts . . . Jo, Joseph? Poolside he'd brought G&Ts which cost eighty pence a go. We would order two at a time back then. Or was that Entebbe? No, Entebbe was the black Father Christmas, his beard unsticking itself in the heat, wishing us white folk around the pool a Merry Christmas, as if there was no problem with the set up. On the railings had sat pink flamingos, eyes on our plates of chips. Red earth made up the roads. Or was that Lusaka? What a mess, I thought, what a fool I was to get my Africas so muddled up.

Whoever and wherever Joseph the pool boy was, he was not employed here anymore. I got up, lifting the thin towels from the loungers – some crew had used three – and dumped them by the disused service stand. I gathered mine round my hips, the material not stretching all the way.

A slapping noise came from the child as he ran round the pool's edge, his hair wet and shining. There was just a wedge of sun left, and the captain and his wife were sat in it. It made me angry, how the day was draining off and there were girls in the orphanage, while we were sat on sun loungers. The wife's blonde hair was pulled up into a messy bunch, she was drinking beer from a tall bottle. My tongue pressed my front teeth; I wanted a drink, of course. But it kept me in the same loop. I didn't have to drink, just because they were. It wasn't a rule – as the sun left – even though it felt like a set rhythm. The wife rough-dried her son's hair, and he sat between her bony knees. I imagined how warm her skin would feel, clamped against his. I smelt my shoulder, the sun mixed in with the lotion. He probably didn't even realise the luck of her easy love.

Slotting my feet into my flip flops, I squeaked across the lawn. Passing the dried-up fountain, I thought of the hotel staff who'd been let go. Nevertheless, the lawn was still green and springy. My thoughts went to Mum and how she was still intending to come away with me, especially now I had free concession tickets. But every time I got rostered a decent trip, something happened with Dad.

Only a couple of months ago, she'd nearly made it as a 'cling-on' with me to Nairobi. We were going on safari to spot elephants, then onto the animal sanctuary where I had stood up a tower to be at the same height as the giraffes. As I stood holding out a handful of feed a giraffe had eyed me up, then sneezed in my face, which I believed was in response to me being the tallest, therefore posing a threat.

We'd decided on Mum's outfit for the plane (lilac wedding suit – in case she was upgraded to business class, she had to appear smart). She'd made Dad portions of shepherd's pie and spaghetti Bolognese for every night she was to be away. She'd even labelled the containers with the nights of the week. They'd discussed what he would do for his lunch, and he was allowed to go to the pub. She had even returned some of the monthly house allowance he gave her to fund this extra cost. But the night before we were going, he slipped down the stairs, knocking his head on the corner of the telephone table. Her new suitcase (first one with wheels) purchased from Debenhams with her savings, which had stood waiting by the door, was then taken back upstairs and unpacked.

I was beginning to believe there was something more to accidents than first met the eye. Steve had fallen over in Baltimore, into the harbour water, which meant he got to take time off work. And this mishap of Dad's was a little too fortuitous. I knew he wasn't mentally unwell enough to stage a fall down the stairs, but I did wonder whether unaddressed emotions created weak spots in the atmosphere which could act like banana skins.

No chance of getting any further with this theory now, I decided. The visit to the orphanage that morning had taken it out of me. Upset yes, but I wasn't prepared for how unsettled I would feel after the visit. Once the initial sadness had subsided, I had expected a warmth inside because I had taken action; instead I was left with a discomfort, a plummeting sensation, something I couldn't get away from.

At the back of the hotel, I passed empty patio bar tables and chairs. The light was leaving us, marking it as time for sundowners. From above came a hoot. Human, not bird. I glanced at the myriad balconies, finding one with its sliding door open, dark like a gap tooth. A crew party no doubt. No one had mentioned it, which is what I wanted wasn't it? To be left alone not to drink? I tried not to feel excluded. Wasn't I the one who had so enjoyed singing 'The Sound of Music' to the crew in Cape Town, and wasn't I the one who pressed my bare breasts against the glass wall in a hotel bar where the whole crew had been drinking? The one who suggested toga parties with hotel room bedsheets? What about that night I'd bobbed naked, my ears submerged in the Ghanaian sea, while two stewards had snogged on the beach under the pulsing stars? Hadn't I worked hard on my reputation of being the flasher, the good-time-girl, the dancing, singing, lover of life who brought the party? And without all this, which was curdling anyhow, what was left?

From the outside the hotel didn't appear in bad repair, but along with the beauty salon, the massage parlour was closed, and the casino now only opened at weekends. I wished I'd said no about going out with the nuns this evening. I could do without spending energy I didn't have. This sagging feeling meant I shouldn't go. The best place for me would be in bed, sunk in one of my long repairing dozes.

That morning I had taken a taxi to the girl's orphanage I'd made contact with, a low crumbling building run by the Sisters of Mercy. A nun named Rozi had opened the door in wire-rimmed spectacles and a blue and white habit. The thin silver pendant of a nailed Jesus to a cross pitched to the side of her bosom.

'Welcome,' Rozi said, showing me through to a large, shaded room, the air heavy with cooked rice.

'Toys, for the children,' I said, offering her the black sack I'd transported from home. She nodded, not opening it to peer inside as I hoped, but propping it against the wall. Recently in the UK, McDonald's had been offering a free stuffed toy with every Happy Meal. Sometimes a Care Bear, or a Disney character like Winnie the Pooh; they were seen as disposable. Mum, who was working back as a dinner lady, had collected them for me from the local parents.

Bettina, the head nun, soon appeared along with a line of girls in over-sized dresses with fraying hems or outdated puff-sleeves. They formed a semi-circle and sang a Zimbabwean song, swaying their hands side to side. *Everybody's happy now, happy now, happy now, we are all beautiful, beautiful, and free.*

This was not the first time I had witnessed a good-natured show put on by orphans, and I knew not to cry, however monumental it felt to be sung to. This was a regular performance for them and was undertaken with the same obedient energy I imagined they used for carrying out chores. I was a white nobody, with money and a GAP striped top. Through their eyes, I signified abundance.

Rozi chatted on as she led me to a room with dusty cream walls. She hoped it would soon have desks and chairs, but for now the children sat on the floor. We passed through dormitories with grey blankets stretched smooth over bunk beds. Then we took an exit to a freshly swept courtyard, where I found a row of toddlers sat quietly on a stretch of material. Each was holding a plastic bowl or had it propped in front of their legs. Two women in headscarves perched on their haunches, delivering porridge into the mouths of those who couldn't hold a spoon. The infants were exceptionally quiet, some gazing up at me with their giant eyes.

The tour continued into a well-tended garden. Rozi informed me they grew what they could, since there was little food at the market. At every turn, I felt an unspoken conversation between us, a nag about whether I would be donating money. I knew there was an economic crisis because we had received information from Scheduling to bring American dollars, as local currency was worth nothing. Arriving yesterday at Harare airport, we were used to being waved through immigration without showing our passports, but this time we were stopped and searched. When my case was opened, I felt embarrassed by the sandwich toaster, loaf of bread, sliced cheese and white onion I'd brought to consume in my room. The crew often 'Delsey dined'. Rumour had it that someone had once successfully fried an egg on a light bulb.

The officers took my food for inspection yet didn't bring it back. They then questioned me about the bag of second-hand children's clothes Mum had collected, as well as the wall clock I'd brought in its original packaging. When I'd explained it was all for the Sisters of Mercy, they nodded and allowed me to shut my case.

We continued past a washing line strung with nappy cloths and then, as the light was slowed by the canopy of a tree, two girls came to swing on a low branch.

'Some of the girls like to sit and pray here,' Rozi said, extending her palm to a series of mounds in the earth. Each one was marked with a homemade cross of twigs bound with twine.

'Are they ...?' I didn't need to finish the sentence. I counted fourteen banks in all.

'Yes. They are our girls,' Rozi said. There was nothing more to say, so we walked to the side, and she talked me through the plants: radish, okra, spinach; an apple tree which needed better soil.

On the way back to the house, I asked Rozi what to bring if I were to get another trip. More clothes, nappies? She shook her head and suggested paracetamol, cough syrup, toothpaste and most startlingly, condoms. The nuns visited the local villages to advise women on contraception, where they rolled them over the ends of bananas. The women laughed; the men stood outside the huts. It was not working, yet I didn't feel it was my place to suggest the nuns should be demonstrating this to the men as well as the women. And when I asked how many people in Zimbabwe had contracted AIDS, she said there were too many to count, too many orphans for orphanages, so they spilled out into the unknown places.

'But here are our girls, alive and learning,' she said, as we returned to the cool of the school room. A group, all different ages, were sat on the swept floor, watching Bettina who was writing the English alphabet on the chalkboard.

'And there are also the boys,' Rozi said, as she walked me back towards the entrance. 'The unaccounted for. Would you like to know about them?'

'Yes,' I said with a croak, then cleared my throat.

'Tonight Bettina and I are off to tend to them. We do this once a month, the boys know to watch for the van. Perhaps you would like to assist?'

'Of course,' I said too quickly, without thinking. 'I'd love that. It must be very interesting.' The words lacked the right inflections; I was sure Rozi noticed.

'You have airline celebrations?'

'No, I'm here to help you.'

'We are thankful for your time.'

Making sure I left a respectable gap before changing the subject, I took out the clock from my bag. Mum no longer wanted it; she had bought it from Marks and Spencer on one of her spending sprees in the sales and I had nearly let her chuck it out. The face was made up of miniature bread loaves marking out the hours. It was so twee, I had not thought it worth carrying all the way over.

'This is for you,' I said, as I offered it to Rozi. 'If you want it.'

She grasped hold of the box, turning it this way and that.

'Oh my,' she ran her finger over the individual loaves and I thought she would put it aside.

'What a gift. It is so very special, beautiful. Thank you, madam. Could I . . .? I don't suppose, well, could I keep it for my sleeping quarters? I have never seen anything like this before.'

'Of course,' I said. And then I noticed Rozi's face as she pulled away the packaging to reveal the whole clock.

'Uh-oh, no batteries,' she said.

'Ah no, I didn't think.'

Rozi turned the clock to face her, then twiddled the back, the hands moving in jolts.

'Eleven o'clock,' she said. 'The time is correct for the way the sun is outside.'

Holding it in front of her, she took a moment, tilting it this way and that.

'I will bring batteries next time, I promise.'

'Next time?'

'Oh yes, I will be back as soon as I can. Or maybe could I post them?'

'Bless you. Then I shall take it to my room, and one day listen to its tick.' Rozi creased up, her hand rushing to block her mouth, as if for a moment she were a girl.

On the way out of the orphanage, I shook Rozi's hand, holding her dry fingers in mine. I imagined coming back with hand cream. Clarins, or at the very least a large tub of cocoa butter, plus a whole bag of batteries.

As I had instructed, the taxi had waited. On the journey back to the hotel, the driver turned off the engine while we sat in traffic. I fantasised how I would do a fun run to raise money. Mum would collect medical supplies and maybe Rozi and I would write to one another, back and forth, me sending her money for stamps. When I returned the girls would run and tug my sleeves then throw their arms round my hips, and I would learn every one of their names.

Now it was dark, the temperature in my hotel room had dropped. I showered the lotion off my skin while thinking how Rozi had not mentioned God once. I found an ancient thermostat on the wall, but when I moved the dial it made no click, and no noise came from the heater.

I sifted through my suitcase and pulled on a t-shirt. Then I found my striped blue-and-white jersey to go over it. I hadn't packed a jumper, not even a light coat, and weighed up whether to wear my pyjama top over both layers, but part of me wanted Rozi to notice the anchor emblem on the breast of the jersey. She liked the detail in things and maybe she would exclaim something about it. Then I would pull off the top, just before we left one another, and pass it to her and say, *here Rozi, this is just for you.*

As I pulled on my jeans, I wondered if Rozi would know what nautical fashion was? The zip hurt my fingers as I tugged it over my belly, and as I leant down to tie up my laces, I told myself discomfort from fat was the least I should endure. It was my punishment for having it all and still being discontented. I checked my watch: quarter to six. The nuns would be downstairs in fifteen minutes. Sliding the hotel notepad in my back pocket, I slotted in a pencil, then squirted on some perfume. As I went downstairs, I tried to rub it off. I didn't want the nuns to think I was flaunting my wealth. Passing the entrance to the dark wooden bar, I could hear music, but the lack of voices meant the crew were yet to congregate.

Out the front of the hotel, beyond the forecourt, it was getting too dark to see. Only one lamp lit the entrance and my breath hung in the air like cigarette smoke. I amused myself for a while, seeing how much breath I could make hang. Accra, Lagos, Lusaka, Cape Town – I never realised anywhere in Africa could be so cold at night.

A bird flew into a tree above. The branches shook, more leaves fell, making me shiver. Rozi had mentioned the windy month of August was when the msasa trees lost their leaves. As I drew close, I made out a bird's hooked beak, the linen white of its feathers. There were a series of thuds from it beating its wings. *What are you?* I thought. I pulled out the pad of paper and wrote down: *black beak, white feathers, yellow feet? = heron?*

I would ask Dad about its features. Placing a chair next to him, I would hand him the pocket RSPB bird book, then I would listen. I would not be scared of him anymore. If we could talk about the heron, the soft man might return. In the daytime he was mostly tucked in the back room with his little TV. High blood pressure now to go with the diabetes. No booze strictly allowed, although we knew he still drank.

The white van drew up and Rozi waved both her hands, smiling like an old friend. Bettina, the head nun, watched from behind the wheel, her eyes gazing coolly ahead. The door was stiff to open, but once in I sank into the back seat. As we journeyed along, I felt every pothole in the road. The nuns spoke among themselves in a low-level murmur I couldn't determine, and I wondered if this was what exhaustion sounded like.

We slowed at the crossroads, then veered right towards the yolky glow of a Shell petrol garage. Parking on a patch of scrubland, the nuns opened the back doors and began to unpack chairs in the weak light of the forecourt. I helped them carry objects to a flat patch of earth, and we went about in a quick business-like manner. Rozi directed me with inserting poles into the sleeves of a marquee, while Bettina positioned a fold-up table in the centre. There was a strong stench in the air and as I inhaled, I remembered Mum's love of diesel. Then I wondered whether the nuns had had their dinner. I was hungry and told myself I could eat later on, but still my eyes kept darting across to the garage, wondering whether there was a shop which sold crisps. I could buy everyone a chocolate bar with the twenty dollars in my pocket.

Bettina brought out two large flasks. I hung three wind-up lanterns from loops around the tent. It was my job to get them to work. Every one minute of winding equalled twenty minutes of light. Rozi laid out a stethoscope, a first aid kit, then a large, scratched biscuit tin, the sort Mum got from work at Christmas.

'How will they know to come?' I asked, wrapping my arms round myself, then stamping my feet in the dust. A smell of burning plastic drifted over. The cars lined up for petrol, some without working front lights.

'They are already here,' Rozi said, pointing towards the lane of traffic. 'Please. You are cold. Wear this.' From a laundry bag, she pulled out a creased white doctor's coat.

'I'm underdressed, sorry,' I said, realising I had created another burden for Rozi. Slotting my arms into the thick material, though the sleeves ruched up and the front did not meet it warmed my back at once.

Soon the shadows of boys came from the road: seven, eight, nine in total. I couldn't see their faces until they reached the tent. Some wore shoes or flip flops, while others went barefoot. I tried not to look at their toenails, or the sores and split skin on their feet. Ankles were the worst;

their small bones appeared so unstable, a miracle they could hold up anyone really. It was the tallest who led, a small woolly Thomas the Tank Engine hat perched on his head. He didn't smile and his eyelids hung heavy. There was no song, no entertainment for me this time. Then he swung his eyes up at me, quickly checking with the nuns to see what was going on.

'Say hello, Thomas,' Bettina said, nodding. 'Our guest has come all the way from the UK.'

'Hello aunty.'

'Thomas, I like your hat,' I said, twitching my fingers towards him, but not extending it into a handshake. He stared with his bloodshot, yellowing eyes, until a long lorry turned into the petrol station, shutting down, hissing loudly. I shivered, but the boy seemed not to react. Rozi offered me a plastic chair, then she sat at the fold-out table and opened a large book. Thomas stood close by, as if he wanted to know me. I turned my knee a fraction away, then forced it back to where it had been. He smelt of chemicals and old sweat, yet I tried not to show him how bad.

'Industrial glue,' head nun Bettina said, when she realised what I was thinking.

I hoped the nuns would advise me on what to do, but they'd become busy holding the boys on the weighing scales, joking while looking in their mouths, then writing it all down. One of the shortest boys edged beside me, his big eyes creased with bags underneath. He was too young to be so tired. He coughed, his lungs crackling with mucus, then reached up to touch my hair. Thomas pushed him roughly back, hissing, and so the boy went to Rozi and the unopened biscuit tin.

'Aunty, are you a doctor?' Thomas asked.

'No, I'm an air stewardess.' I caught myself wondering if he would know about airlines, then stopped, because he had eyes, and of course there was a sky with planes here. Word surely would have got through about the Twin Towers, or the stowaways who kept trying to get to London from Africa by wrapping themselves round the landing gear.

'How old are you Thomas?'

'The nuns say I am eleven.'

He spoke softly, and when he rested his fingers on my arm, I let them stay there. Although he was big compared to the others, I realised he was not nearly tall enough for his age. Pearly white spots grew at side of his mouth, a sign of HIV. When I had been to the AIDS orphanage in Nairobi, a malnourished seven-year-old, the size of a large toddler, had sat running a Smartie around in urine on the floor with the same beaded face. Again, I felt the skin around my hips wince, just as I had that time, clenching as a shield against their pain. But I couldn't put my hand on top of his, however much I knew I should, like Lady Di once had with the AIDS patients in hospital. Instead, I stopped breathing through my nose and opened my mouth.

'Where do you live?' he asked.

'England.'

'Manchester United?'

'You like football?'

'Oh yes, madam. We play. We have a ball. Made of a rice bag. I want to be a footballer. Or a scientist.'

'Ingenious.' The word flew out of nowhere, a good smart word.

'In genius,' he repeated, enjoying it. He stepped forward, mesmerised, or was he in a trance? Whichever, he came close.

Then I made myself touch his hand, now resting on my knee as light as an envelope.

'I think maybe you are a doctor? With your medicine coat?'

'Oh, this?' I felt the collar. 'No, but I do know first aid.'

'You have been to university? In England?'

'Yes, well, Wales.' He looked perplexed.

'It's part of Britain. I went a long time ago now,' I laughed, starting to enjoy myself, as if I were the kind of person who could say, *Oh that old time!* I realised, this could be easier than I thought. If I let it. I could work for UNICEF. Amnesty International. Was this my true life coming for me?

'I studied art. Nothing that useful I'm afraid.'

'Drawing? You have pencils? And pens? All I need is a pen. If I have one, I can go to school.'

'I do. Here,' I pulled out the pencil from my back pocket, and then the hotel note pad. The other boys turned, then began to crowd round, looking around me for more.

'I've only got one, for now. But there are plenty at the hotel.'

'Ssh,' Bettina said, and she shook her head. 'You must not tell the boys things like this.'

I felt I had been insensitive. I thought of all those hotel pens I'd collected, now stood in the 'I heart Chicago' mug back home in London. I thought of all the drawings I could have done over the years of flying but had not done. All the notebooks I never took the wrapper off from stationary shops, piling up in the dark waiting for my courage, my will. To stop waiting.

Thomas moved closer and sniffed my perfume. I smiled at him.

167

'There was a man, he took my square of soap,' he said.

'Oh.'

'With no soap I cannot wash my clothes.'

'I see.'

'And with no clean face, and no pencil, I cannot go to school. Doctor? Will you sponsor me?'

'Thomas,' Rozi said. 'Ssh now please child.'

'I don't know if I can . . .' I said, searching over at Rozi who shook her head. Even so, there was something in her eyes, waiting for me to decide what I was going to do. Why was I here? I thought of my credit card, how I owed thousands of pounds from shopping round the world, buying all the needless clothes and things for my flat. How I was obsessed with balance transfers, finding the latest zero interest rates, swapping my debt over, never getting to the bottom of why I had created it.

After a while, Rozi spoke. 'Thomas, come here and be weighed, please.' Then she opened the tin and the boys jostled into a queue for biscuits. Two were counted out for every child and of course, I didn't take the one offered to me.

Black tea was served in plastic beakers with lumps of sugar. The boys' height and weight measurements were entered into the ledger alongside their names and approximate birth years, with any new ailments listed in a separate column. At every moment the nuns hugged and touched the boys. It was far from depressing. After this, Thomas returned and I let him rest his hip against my knee, both of us not moving, while I calculated how much I would give the nuns.

'Aunty, I will look for you tomorrow morning. I know where the airline van heads for the airport. We watch it go by every Tuesday and Thursday.' Then he touched my cheek and for a few seconds, I hung my arm loosely round his waist.

When the nuns started offering the broken ends of biscuits, Thomas joined the other boys. As I got up, I realised I'd grown stiff with cold. The boys played a game with sticks as Rozi started to dismantle the marquee, and I felt relieved we would be leaving. At first viewing the marquee had seemed so elaborate and new, but now as I helped pack it up, I noticed spots of mildew and rips. I helped enthusiastically with the slotting together of the poles and the boys lingered, helping fetch and carry everything to the van.

Bettina said goodbye individually to each of the boys, holding their shoulders firmly while telling each of them she loved them. Then she climbed behind the wheel and put on the headlights, waiting. Rozi gave each of the boys an embrace, then slammed the back door, brushing her hands together so they made the noise of sandpaper. I waved as the boys wandered off, and Rozi came alongside me to watch their outlines move to the side of the road. The traffic had died down now and each of them bent over to pick up bits of cardboard, dragging it after them.

'Time to go,' Rozi said. As I began for the van, I glanced back. The boys were dipping into the earth, their arms pulling the cardboard over their heads.

'What are they doing?' I said.

'They are going to bed,' Rozi said. 'To sleep. There's a ditch in the centre.'

'But the traffic?'

'It is the safest place. Away from the men.'

She must have noticed the look on my face because she sighed, then started to explain.

'Everyone is only capable of doing so much. God works in this way. Good will come. Small things add up to larger movements.' She nodded up at the sky, and I followed her gaze to the crescent moon, a white earring sharp enough to hang some hope off it.

Only a few cars were driving from the centre now, but the drivers would know there were boys sleeping not far from their tyres. If only I could be as blind, close my eyes now and forget what I'd seen. I realised how the boy's lives counted for nothing. Not even enough for the government to make it law to have their births officially registered.

Before Rozi and Bettina left me at the hotel, I promised to return with supplies on my next trip. In that moment I passionately believed I would. There was a chance I could be rostered another trip next month. This pleased them, and Rozi thanked me, but they were tired and must go. Now I'd said it, I suspected my words lacked the momentum needed to make something long lasting happen. There were rumours the airline was pulling out of Zimbabwe. Since the collapse of the economy, the political unrest and the ousting of the white farmers, it would be impossible to make it a profitable route. This is what it came down to for the airline in the end, profit and loss.

'Here, please take this.' I handed over a twenty dollar note.

'Thank you,' Rozi smiled. She passed it to Bettina, who bowed her head.

As I watched the van signal from the hotel, it drove off fast, the one taillight blinking as if they couldn't get away quick enough. Perhaps they were relieved to see the back of all the wealth, and all I stood for. I wanted to pull away from all of it too.

The automatic doors didn't part when I stood in front of the sensor, so I pushed open the side door. It was warm inside the lobby, and I noticed my shoulders drop. Crossing the wide marble floor, past the sculptures of plump rhinos, thinking of Mum, taking in the chandeliers high above, I nodded at the bellboy behind his desk. I could hear raised voices along with a percussion band in the bar. I crossed by the café, with the cake display fridge empty and switched off. A large group of smartly dressed locals piled from a side room. A waiter in a black waistcoat and white shirt held a tray of wine. An art exhibition was on show, and I peered into the room at the abstract paintings. The boys in the ditch were only ten minutes away, but they might well have been right on my shoulder. I longed to yell, *wake up, wake up!* If I were a different kind of person, more like the person I thought I would be with my shaved head from art college, I would call out the injustice.

Instead, on the way to the lift, I recognised a woman coming from the toilets. Sarah with the full lips and wavy blonde hair. I'd tried my first vodka martini with her during tornado season in Miami. She came over, holding her purse, a look of delight spreading across her face. Her nose was burnt red, and her off the shoulder top showed a bikini line. Her eyes were such a true blue, I'd quite forgotten until now.

'Gosh, I haven't seen you for an age. How are you? You look well. Have you been out jogging?' she said, running her hand over my arm, the alcohol acrid on her breath.

'No.' I felt my face. 'I've been out with a nun's outreach programme. The boys, they have to sleep by the road. It's sickening.' My words trembled out and I felt very angry with her, as if she were responsible.

'That's terrible,' Sarah said. 'But such is life over here. I brought out some used trainers for the bellboy.'

'You did?'

'Yep, his face when I gave them. I could just melt.' She glanced at the bar. 'You coming? Karaoke with a live band. Our captain has just sung "I Will Survive" wearing lipstick. He's such a bloody laugh for a "Nigel".'

I peeped over her shoulder into the bar, jostling with life.

'No, I don't think so, not tonight.'

'Oh, come on, you're the party. Remember how those palm tree leaves raced by us in the winds on the streets of Miami? We were searching for any open bar? I told my mum how you'd said, "If we're going to die, let's die drinking a Martini!" And she said you sounded like a right laugh. Like a kind of femme fatale.' The flattery was intended to seduce, and for the first time ever, I heard it and didn't trust it. It was the booze talking through Sarah, alcohol searching out my company, trying to light the flame.

'Oh, I probably smell a bit,' I said, sniffing my armpits.

'Aw, come on. You can't stay in. Not here.'

'I'm not . . .'

'But it's so rare to be in the same place at the same . . .'

'I suppose I could get showered and . . .'

'That's the spirit. Right, see you in twenty then?' Sarah said. 'What you drinking?'

I laughed a little forced laugh.

'Don't worry,' I said, 'I'll decide when I come down.'

Inside my room, proud of my resolve, I found my mobile and switched it on, hoping for a text from someone back home. Steve was in Thailand on holiday with a new man. I thought to message Mum, so she would send me a message back, but what would I write? She was so wrung out with Dad, and it would upset her to know I was out with the homeless boys smelling of glue. Would she even understand why I'd been with them? Why *had* I? It wasn't going to change anything. There was a part of me who wanted to give them all my money, but there was also a part who knew it was a drop in the ocean, that it was about making me feel better.

Everyone is only capable of doing so much, Rozi had said.

I slumped on the bed and pressed the keys on the phone:

Hi Mum, been out with homeless boys and nuns.
Awful. Feel so sorry for them, wish I was home. How's
Dad? XXX

Putting on the shower to run hot, I switched on the TV and flicked to BBC World News. There was a programme about Japan and its economy. How there was a job for everyone whatever their age. An elderly Japanese man was being interviewed. He stood all day at the bottom of the escalator, holding a cloth to the handrail on the Tokyo metro system, as it ran by underneath. He was thankful for it. His words translated as, 'without work, life has no purpose.'

A minute later my phone beeped:

Oh dear how sad. Maureen has a pair of shoes high
heeled sized 7 wonder if you would like them x

I slumped down wondering if a glass of wine would actually help. Then I forced my mind to the kettle, remembering how the milk for my tea, the tea which could taste like back home, had been taken from my bag at the airport. I composed a text to Steve:

Been out with outreach programme with some nuns.
Truly awful, but considering sponsoring a young boy.
Thomas. How are you? Been missing you, love, your
gal xxxxx

Of course, there was no reply. The time change for Koh
Samui was the same as Bangkok. Five hours ahead from
here, he was probably in bed. I thought about texting Mum
back about the shoes because she would then text back.
I pictured her in front of the TV, glancing at her phone,
waiting for my reply. I knew this picture off by heart, as if
we were connected by a wire.

On the bathroom rack there were two thin stiff towels.
I showered then wiped the steam from the mirror to study
my face. I stared at it so long I no longer recognised it as a
whole thing. Trying a smile for Sarah, I then looked at my
teeth. One was yellowing from smoking. Thomas's touch
was still on my hand, and I sniffed the skin to check. Sat in
the curved dip of the sink was the usual bar of complimentary soap in its wrapper. Every hotel room around the world
offered one. Millions of bars waiting in the dips of sinks, in
boxes in store rooms, enough to give one to every living
street kid. I pulled off the wrapper, then turned on the tap.
Glad for the comfort of hot water, I rinsed my hands over
and over, lathering the soap. Vague perfume, not great suds.
When I replaced it on the sink, I decided not to go to the
bar. I would take the room phone off the hook and write
in my notebook.

The room service menu only offered a few options. My
eyes jumped quickly from 'soup of the day' to 'club sandwich with chips'. I calculated the price would be twenty
pounds including a tip. Thomas needed thirty pounds a

month to go to school. He'd told me this with such deep longing, wanting only what was taken for granted at home. It had given me a perspective I didn't know what to do with.

Shaking my head to change the atmosphere about me, I pressed 9 for room service. The voice at the other end apologised, they had no sandwiches tonight. I quickly ran my finger down the menu and settled on spaghetti Bolognese. Surprisingly they confirmed the order, which meant they had pasta, probably imported from Italy or from the States at great expense.

Opening my wheelie bag I remembered how the airport officers hadn't been interested in the miniature white wines. I cracked open a bottle: warm, unpleasant. Not wanting it, still I drank more. But the feeling of being carried off did not start.

The street below was empty when I checked. I hoped to catch a glimpse of Thomas, but there was nothing but whistling wind. I drank a second bottle on the bed, pushing on, hoping to leave the misery. When there was a knock at the door, I opened it to find the room service waiter. I thought of Sarah and the trainers she'd brought and wondered if I should give him my Converse. He might have a wife, or a sister. I directed him to place the tray on the bed, then gave him the usual dollar tip. He folded it into his trouser pocket, and I said, 'jambo' brightly, and he replied 'jambo' quickly.

'How are you?' I asked.

'Good, thank you madam.' His hair was shaped nicely on top.

'I went out with the orphan boys earlier. Have you heard of the street boys?'

'Yes, madam.'

'I . . .do you . . . How do you think I could best help?

You know, what do you think is the best way? I have trainers, I've barely worn them. And some socks. And this sandwich toaster.' I ran to my suitcase, opened it up, started unpacking everything. I found the shoes and held them out in front of me. They had cost me nearly nothing in the States.

'They are a little scuffed on the toe, but they're still good?'

'We are not permitted to accept gifts from guests.'

'Are you not?'

'Yes, it is hotel policy. So, if that's all madam?'

'I could write a note, say I want to give them to you?'

'Please, I am fine, thank you madam.'

He turned for the door. A two-inch gap ran from the bottom of his trousers to the back of his shoes. His socks were thatched bare, a potato shape on his heel. When the door clicked behind him, I sat on the bed cross-legged, going over why he had not taken the shoes when Sarah said she'd given hers away so easily.

Lifting up the silver dome plate cover, the meat was grey and there were red globules of tomato sauce floating in oily water. It smelt of nothing and the portion was small. As I forked through there were no mushrooms. Not even a salt and pepper sachet.

Eat it, I instructed. I flicked out the stiff napkin, then scooped meat onto the fork. As I ran it round my mouth, my tooth met something hard. So I spat it out and upon examining it, sifted out a bit of bone. Saliva rushed round, but I knew I had to finish the meal. There was no way I could put the tray outside the door half eaten. I'd become the story of the fortunate white stewardess who carries her own sandwich toaster, then refuses to eat the food. I twisted the spaghetti round the fork, forming a bundle, then put it in my mouth, making myself swallow the strings.

It was while watching an old Madonna video, *Vogue*, that I felt shivery, as if someone had walked over my grave. I went into the bathroom, my stomach making absurdly loud guttural noises. Sitting on the edge of the bath, I wished I could be at home in my flat. I could smell bleach and noticed a dirty mark under the toilet bowl. Feeling a bubbling sensation, I tasted bile, but held it back; I would not put my fingers down my throat to aid this self-induced sickness.

For the next hour I vomited, rushing to the bathroom, then shuddered back under the covers. I tried taking tablets, but they wouldn't stay down. The hours stretched around me. Time clicked in the bulb of the lamp when I turned it off, the fridge came on with a surging buzz, then would stop dead. This hotel room was unfriendly. Over the years I had learnt to doze off by emergency exit doors, upright chairs in crew rest, I could power nap on sofas, coaches, airport lounges; so why wouldn't it let me sleep here?

It was the early hours when I heard the doors slamming as crew returned from the bar. I imagined walking round my flat back home, from the lounge to the corridor, then in the lift to the communal gardens, with the roses and sheds, picturing the car port lights flick on to the paused foxes. The more boring the mind-walk the better. Mum and Dad would be in bed down the road, so I went there, listening to Dad's snores vibrating the walls. The L Gang would be in their flats, work tomorrow, then gearing up for the weekend. We were going to a club off Leicester Square. I said I would provide the vodka, as usual concealed in my bra, one size too big.

Still, it was no good. Sleep refused entry. Then the gale outside began shoving the window. Wind was a worry, the weather, it had the power to undo. My eyes wide open, I remembered sachets of peppermint tea tucked in my handbag from Riyadh where we were made to wear abayas on leaving the plane. I boiled mineral water in my travel kettle, then sat on the edge of the bed, sipping the hot drink, watching the night sky refuse to budge. Every so often, the trees whined.

I decided to watch a pay-on-demand movie. Most of the titles were years old: *Crocodile Dundee, Calendar Girls, Alien* – I needed something I hadn't seen before, so I chose *The Good Girl* starring Jennifer Aniston. It was easy to pretend I knew her, and although some saw her as anodyne, I thought she was a good comic actress. Besides, I might laugh or cry, and I knew both of those things might act as a mooring, a purging, in the night.

When the familiar roar of the lion started, I turned up the volume to mask the blustery gales outside. Soon I became submerged in the story; I was taken in by the part where Jennifer meets a store boy who thinks he's a character from a novel, when suddenly the TV turned itself off. The hotel room blinked to black.

Blindly, I touched along surfaces until I came across the shape of my phone. By the light of the Nokia I found the door handle. The corridor was lit with green emergency lighting, and I was reassured the hotel was having a power cut. I'd experienced these before in Africa. Often there was a short gap before the generator kicked in, so I got back under the covers, and waited. I ran through my money situation and did the sums of what I'd earnt since arriving in Zimbabwe, then deducted what I'd spent. Adding the room service meal to the half-watched movie, the taxi to and from the orphanage, the twenty dollars donation, I'd spent more money than it would cost to sponsor Thomas for three months of schooling.

I must have dozed because when I next opened my eyes, the lights were on, and the sky was lavender-grey. I switched off the lamps then waited for the sunrise to find the tops of the trees. Still feeling dreadful, I pulled a sheet of hotel paper from the padded desk folder. There was no way I could work home. My forehead *was* a little hot. I decided to write to my manager and say I was sick, how I'd been up all night. When finished I stood in front of the wardrobe mirror and rubbed my forehead, to see how well I acted out pain.

On the way to the manager's room to deliver the note, I limped along, swallowing as if my throat were swollen. Practising the voice, weaker than mine in case I happened upon any early rising crew, I said, 'No, not too good I'm afraid.'

When the manager woke to find my note pushed under his door, I understood he would not want to work one crew member down, nor would he want to do all the paperwork or call operations at Heathrow. So when the phone rang, I knew it was him. Still, I persisted, I was too sick to work, food poisoning from the hotel room service, plus a temperature, but of course I was well enough to position home, and I would see a doctor on my return.

Later in reception at pick up, the crew filed onto the bus, and I held back, dressed in a pair of black trousers and my jersey shirt but no makeup, in case it made me appear too healthy. On the drive towards the airport, the bus stopped at the crossroads by the Shell garage from the night before. In daylight it was a dry patch of land, litter covering the worn-away grass. Before I realised it was him, Thomas's woollen hat caught my eye. Now it was day I saw his nostrils were caked with dried mucus. It appeared he was looking for me, and he sprang forward at the side of the van, patting my window with his palm. Opening the glass, however glad I was to see him, I still had to act unwell for the crew.

'Doctor! Madam.'

'Thomas, how are you?' I whispered in a way I could maintain my illness, while expressing the absolute joy at seeing him again. I turned to face the van's interior, announcing, 'These boys are homeless. Do we have anything to give them? Money? Food?'

Keeping a fifty dollar note hidden, I pulled out a ten dollar note, then made it twenty. There was a general flurry about the van as out came pens, apples, bananas, packets of biscuits, nuts, and dollars and I fed it through the window before the lights changed. Other boys appeared, their hands reaching up.

As the bus moved off, I heard them, 'Madam, madam!' but I could not look back. I had to hold it together, so I pressed my forehead as if my eyes hurt.

The crew left me in the departure lounge where I was to wait for my boarding pass. I wanted to go to the duty free shop to buy the six pound bottle of vodka but knew this wasn't the action of an ill stewardess.

The gold and silver card holders exaggerated their status by bustling to the front of the queue, making sure they were ahead of economy passengers. They elongated their necks, all the while pretending they weren't aware of how they were displaying their status. If this was success, they could keep it.

On boarding I was upgraded to a business class seat. On any other day I would've been overjoyed, but as airline staff we were told by management to decline any add ons such as the quality slippers and wash bag. Meanwhile the crew had to pretend I was a regular customer, omitting parts of the service covertly, so paying business class passengers didn't feel short-changed. I think I stood out a mile.

After take-off, I suspected the crew believed I was a fraud by the way they offered me the breadbasket only once. We all knew the service backwards, how it stipulated a choice of bread roll with the tray, again after serving the hot breakfast, then a final choice of sweet pastry. After all the real passengers had their meal, they offered me a leftover vegetarian omelette. I drank water, performing tiny sips, timing them to be in eyeshot of the crew. Even so, before they removed my tray from my table, I secreted the box of designer truffles down the side of the seat. Then I reclined my bed flat, laying on one side, pulling the blanket over my ear. Only when the pain started in my hip did I feel I'd administered the right amount of punishment to turn over. Not once did I dare pull out the in-flight entertainment screen. And still I felt the air of mistrust from the crew every time they passed.

During the cruise, when the first set of crew disappeared on their break, I found a window of freedom. So I pulled back my blanket, opened the overhead locker and retrieved my bag. In my notebook alongside the description of the bird for Dad, I wrote:

Harare: I forgot the batteries. Street boys. They need pens, I have limitless pens. No words, all feelings, I need words to start taking shape. Help! Each time I think, I go blank. Is it time to shoot out an emergency flare? And if so, who do I want to answer it? What is the use of airline training now I'm having a personal emergency?

Then I dared write what I was most scared of.

Is it possible to have a breakdown and not know it? And is a breakdown exactly that, a breaking down of everything you once held true about yourself? I thought it would be more like being in a straitjacket in an asylum, licking the walls. Not something you could hide, while imitating a saner you.

From that day on I began to write sober words and rip the film off all those untouched notebooks. As a kind of artistic and fatherly anchor I lugged 658 pages of Alan Bennett's *Untold Stories* in my suitcase around the globe. I'd felt an affinity with him since watching Thora Hird in 'A Cream Cracker Under the Settee' in his *Talking Heads*. Each time I opened his book in a new hotel room, the words soothed and amused like a self-mooring, clicking on my brain, albeit through stories of his Mam and Dad. Then into the netted underwear area of my case, I slotted Julia Darling's novel, Crocodile Soup – so alive and full of poetry and humour about lesbian love, the sentences leapt from the page. It made me want to write. It told me I must write.

While my suitcase was perpetually thrown into the hold with the poor panting dogs and crates of mangoes, these would be the items held fast. While crossing the world's oceans, I imagined their words infusing my socks and bras, waiting until I got down route when they would then infiltrate my skin, travelling through my veins, stimulating my heart.

CHAPTER 9

In The Wings

PHX – Tucson – PHX – LHR

It was decided. The quickest route to Tucson was via Interstate 10 from Phoenix. Steve and I dumped our uniforms in our rooms at the crew hotel, packed overnight bags, then picked up a silver hire car from Hertz. Steve drove, while I sat in the passenger seat unwrapping butter candies which he nuzzled off my hand. I traced the highway on the map, following the road with my pen beyond Tucson to exotic places like Santa Rosa, then further still on to El Paso and Nogales.

'It's not that far into Mexico you know,' I said, yearning to go back.

'Another time my sweet, we've just the one night.' He was weary, so we stopped at a gas station for coffee and a sweaty pack of doughnuts. As we journeyed along, to keep up our spirits, I pointed out unusual road signs like: ADULTERY

IS ILLEGAL or the 1–800 number for SHOOTING TIPS. For a long spell we sat in silence listening to country music between adverts on the radio.

'Tell me how far you've got with your story then?' Steve said.

'I can't remember,' I said, knowing I'd got to the bit where one main character had to do something to break the everyday pattern. It wasn't lost on me that this was what I was hoping for in life. That I was living so I could tell odd stories of this living. I'd seen a scholarship advertised in a magazine for a writing retreat. All you needed to do was submit a story of a thousand words about, of all things, air. I had just under four months to get something into shape.

'I'm hoping for an American spark,' I said. 'Somehow, if I could weave in something like when I was chased by that wild boar on that Sedona bush trail. How I never knew I could run so fast. How I felt like I was taking off I was so scared.'

'Write that then.'

'Not sure it's natural feeling.'

'Well, so far this road trip hasn't been exactly inspirational,' Steve said. 'Where's that long Arizonan desert road I thought we'd be on? The one in *Thelma and Louise*?'

'They actually shot that scene in Utah.'

'Oh,' Steve said. 'That's not fair.'

Ugly scrubland and cheerless offramp villages passed the window. When a Border Patrol vehicle slowed alongside, the officer, his face the pallor of raw turkey, stared in and Steve quickly decelerated. Jittery with fatigue, we primed ourselves – there was vodka in the boot, perhaps gay porn in Steve's bag. After a minute, the officer decided against whatever he was thinking, and sped off into the fast lane.

A ridge had formed across my knee from being pressed against the glove compartment. This zoned out feeling, I'd learnt, had a name – place lag – the gap in time where your body took time to wholly *arrive* back to itself. Our bodies were not built for such speed, to arrive across the Earth from home to here so quickly, then onto somewhere else without staying long enough to settle on local time.

Suddenly the grey banks lining the freeway flattened to reveal a plain of saguaro cacti, and I felt it, what I had been waiting for.

'This is the place,' I said.

Snow-peaked mountains formed the backdrop to the tall cacti fingers shooting from the earth. A choke of tears came out of the blue. These solitary cactuses were so self-sufficient, strong and other-worldly. The arms of the saguaro grew in such a way to balance itself; if one arm got too heavy, another would sprout the other side to keep the plant stable. Survival, equilibrium and growth was innate to their nature. Yet to humans, this took such effort. I remained quiet. I didn't want to put Steve off the driving with these thoughts. Instead, I watched out the window, thinking about the energy humming in the distant red rocks. On previous trips to Sedona, I'd seen how twisted juniper trees marked where the ley lines crossed – this was why there were so many UFO sightings here. This was why the place promised magic, and I had a lot of time for the unexplained.

When the turn off for Tucson appeared, Steve momentarily dithered about how to get off the freeway. He indicated, but because of his inexperience of driving in the US, swerved dangerously across two lanes. I kept my eyes closed until the car slowed down. Then we passed Mexican restaurants, shop fronts for tax services and a row of dilapidated houses with dusty plastic toys in the yard. The streets widened as we approached a more well-kept neighbourhood, the houses painted in earth colours. Finding where we were on the map, I spotted the red number of the Motel 6 Quality Inn up ahead.

'Steve, on the left.' As we turned in, I spied a group of Latinos getting out of their cars with cool boxes.

'There might be a fiesta,' I said, as Steve concentrated on finding a space nearest reception.

'I hope so, I could do with a livener-upper,' he said.

'Me too,' I said, wondering if I could stick to mostly Diet Coke. Just pretend I was mixing in vodka on this trip.

Outside the car we shook out our stiff knees while the warm desert air met our faces. The motel was straight out of all the motel movies, low rise with a series of doors and a connecting balcony. A musky smell of citrus with an undernote of worn socks hung in the air. Steve stretched out his arms and his t-shirt rose to reveal the smallest of paunches. He pulled it down self-consciously, while I rubbed my nose warm from the car's intense air con.

It was two in the morning back home, six in the evening here. Cicadas pulsed out from the bushes. In the sky there was just a hook of a moon, and a bright glowing light to the side. Waiting for it to move, expecting it to be a low aircraft, it didn't budge. A star. I felt proud to have found a place where the sky might be just as it had looked for centuries. I gently pushed the passenger door shut, nervous about damaging the hire car.

'It's not quite shut,' Steve said.

'Oh right.' I flipped up the handle of the door, then slammed it hard.

'I didn't mean break it,' he said.

'It just came out my hand.'

He turned and pulled his bag from the boot, then yanked out mine. It wasn't like him to be snippy with me. We needed a drink, to be what we were together, but this was the trap. We only had twenty-four hours before going back to Phoenix for pick up. I wanted to be unleashed from all habit, to get to take in the desert light. Be free. I was worried to tell Steve about not wanting to drink in case it made me different to the person I always was with him. This break somehow risked me losing him.

'Sorry, I'm knackered. Need to have a rest,' Steve said.

'We could stay in?' I said. 'Watch a film. Drink root beer in our underpants.'

'Maybe,' he said. 'It seems a shame to stay in though, on the one night here.'

The lobby was basic. Two vending machines, four peach doctor's waiting room-style chairs, plus a stand with twenty-four-hour coffee. It was nothing like the Hilton we'd left in 'Mormon Mesa'. I'd never stayed in a motel before and had wanted to for so long, but the desk went unattended and on the counter was a small sign: 'ring bell'. Steve picked it up, tinkling it. I wandered out front, taking in the pink hue of the sunset over the mountains. A distant sound of voices came from the side of the motel. The group of Latinos were gathering by an adobe building.

'Where you going? It's vodka o'clock,' Steve called, raising the duty free bag.

'Just a few minutes,' I said. 'Meet you back at the pool?'

He nodded and this was my time. Grabbing my rucksack I headed past the hire car and ran my hand over the warm bumper. I strode past the gated pool and counted the cacti along the drive. Six, seven ...ten. A towering palm, its leaves trimmed, reached as high as the motel sign. I stopped to admire how the horizon ran so far from left to right.

Across the street the last of the sun painted the buildings a warm terracotta. There was little traffic on this stretch of road, and I hung back, watching the Latino group form a semi-circle. A small piece of wood with the painted words, *El Tiradito – The Wishing Shrine* was nailed to a post. The people began placing objects on a low table covered in red cloth. One by one, the group chanted out something loud. After a few minutes there was some coughing and a woman with a ponytail pressed her face onto a man's shoulder.

They crossed themselves before heading towards the cool boxes.

'Hello. Excuse me?' I said, heading over, bringing out my notepad from my bag. I fixed my face, lifting the muscles in my cheeks with a disarming airline smile.

'Yes?' One of the women said, jutting up her chin. 'You a reporter?'

'No, I'm an air hostess,' I said, using the outdated term on purpose, knowing it provided me with a certain status. As the woman furrowed her brow, I peered down at my checked shirt, turned up jeans, my dusty Converse trainers.

'Turistas,' she muttered to the group.

I slunk back. What had I expected? They were under-taking a private ritual. I'd read the part in *Lonely Planet ARIZONA* about Tucson once being under Mexican rule. A war in the 19th Century had moved the borders, so the United States then claimed the land as its own. And now migrants were crossing the border to get to the very land which had once been theirs. Sometimes Border Police helped them get registered, but if not they headed into the desert under their own steam, often to die of thirst or hunger.

Walking away from their lives, all those stories, I entered the car park and inspected the back of a dusty pickup truck. I wasn't ready to be with Steve yet. I knew he would be waiting, preparing the glasses, the ice, setting up the night ahead. This was part of a bigger complicated problem. So, I dawdled in the car park, finding a prickly pear cacti and how the buds were about to flower. I thought to get my camera. Mum would never have seen a cacti with fingers. Perhaps she never would. Maybe it was better not to know the things you've missed.

A splashing came from the pool. All I wanted was to sit with the plants. Here I wanted space and time on my terms, if only for one night. The same with the airline, the rosters were always tugging at me, filling in my future, reminding me I had no autonomy under their employment. How I was just a number.

The motel walls were now coffee-cream, the sun almost gone. By the pool gate, I watched Steve swim a few breast-strokes, then relax into a doggy-paddle. A bag of alcohol was propped on a sun lounger with paper coffee cups full of ice. He'd brought down my swimsuit and laid it flat on the lounger. Immediately, I felt sorry. He was a kind, thought-ful man who cared for me. He'd replaced all the lack, and I owed him my loyalty at the very least.

Pulling the towel around me, I dropped my shorts on the ground, yanked my costume up to my waist, letting my breasts feel the night air without worrying who might see. Then as I stepped into the water, Steve swam over. A few midges floated on the surface, and I flicked them away. We swam in a circle, round one another, then I dropped back so my ears went under the surface. Listening to the nothing, while noticing the stars prick out, Steve pulled my ankles and dragged me round softly in a circle, so my hair floated like seaweed.

After, we sat on the loungers wrapped in towels. Steve poured Blue Smirnoff and I drank, slowing myself by counting sips. Each one reminded me how I loved the feeling, taking me off and away. Each sip told me not to be so serious, no one liked the serious side of me, except me. By the time we'd finished half a litre, the counting was replaced by want, by the drink's want for us to be consumed, so we went up to the room.

Inside were two beds with tightly tucked flower-stamped bedspreads. The porch light was on, creating a bourbon glow and I sat bouncing on the bed, not lying back. Steve went about his ritual of personalising the room, unpacking his pillow with its brushed cotton case, then switching it for the one on the bed. He shook out a waffle bathrobe then took out his travel speaker, new iPod and pressed play. He lit a lavender travel candle and disappeared into the bathroom, clanking toiletries along the bathroom shelf.

After a while I heard the shower, so I unpacked my going-out jeans and moved about the room in time to the music, then topped up my cup. Steve appeared in his dressing gown and took out the khaki shirt I liked. We dressed, had a chat about the unions and how they were calling a strike, then ordered a taxi to downtown Tucson.

It wasn't far to the gay bar, IBT's. We sat on barstools, ordering double vodkas and Diet Cokes. Steve hoped someone half decent would walk in and so kept looking behind me every time the door opened. He had finished with his last boyfriend after they'd got caught up in a messy threesome.

At nine o'clock a drag queen took the stage and lip synced to 'Ain't No Mountain High Enough' by Diana Ross. Then a DJ played and Steve and I danced near a couple of local students. When the DJ clocked off, we slotted dimes into the juke box. At eleven o'clock, I leant against the wall and stayed there, feeling brilliant and far away. The bar had emptied, and Steve now watched the bar man. It was a weeknight, and I told him nothing much would happen now, so we hailed a taxi and rode the short trip back, getting the driver to stop for jumbo chilli dogs at a place called Pat's.

Back at the motel we took the stairs. Outside, chairs were positioned by every door, and I fetched a second one from along the way. We shoved down the hot dogs and fries.

'Let's have a night cap,' I said, and went into the room for the vodka.

'Here you go.' I said, handing a shot of vodka, no ice, to Steve.

'I think I'll call it a night,' he said.

'Why?' I drank mine but couldn't feel the hum in it without Steve.

'Driving the hire car tomorrow.'

'When have you become so sensible?'

'I don't always want to, you know . . .'

'What?'

'You know. Drink.'

I wondered if he had read my thoughts and was mirroring how I'd felt earlier.

'Let's go to the wishing shrine,' I said, standing up.

'Where?'

'Come on. Please. I need to go, for the story.'

I dragged his arm until he relented and locked our door. I held my notebook in one hand and pen in the other.

As we crossed the car park, I did the arm movements of an intrepid explorer, as if I held walking sticks. Steve was pondering for a while before saying, 'What I don't get is how you know how to write. I mean, where does it come from?'

'It comes from here,' I said, pointing to my gut. 'Why have you stopped drinking tonight, really?'

'Because of the driving.'

'There's something else going on, isn't there?'

'No, there's not,' he said, sounding annoyed and I felt like he was lying, because he was worse than me. He had been the one earlier to make us drink.

On the table of the shrine, only a couple of tall prayer candles still burned. Printed on the sides were pictures of saints, the insides of the holders blackened. I ran my finger over the subtle ridges in the ink, round the halo of the saint. Across the table were offerings of unopened bottles of beer, plastic sunflowers, a girl's hairbrush. Pinned to a board were countless curled and faded photographs of children, men and women, all with neatly brushed hair. People looking their best for occasions.

Steve held back, as I picked up the hairbrush.

'I had one like this once,' I said, inspecting it. 'Do you wonder if, who you once were is still there waiting, watching?'

There was silence. Then a truck drove by.

'You know any day now,' he said. 'You'll go in too deep.'

His face was grave.

'What do you mean?'

'With all your writing. You'll become rich and famous, then,' he dipped his head. 'Want to leave me.'

'I doubt it, Steve. I've only ever managed short bits.'

'I didn't say it to make you feel bad.'

'I know,' I said. 'I'm sorry. Come here you.' And I pulled him close. 'You think,' I said softly. 'What if we stopped, you know, drinking so much? Do you ever think we have a problem?'

After a while he said, 'No, never.'

He let go of me and searched for a cigarette.

'Shall we head back then, it's late,' he said.

'I think I want to stay, just for a moment more. We're always going round on a hamster wheel. I want time to just stand still.'

'I know you do.'

I felt the tears come. He told me not to cry and I knew I shouldn't because this was supposed to be our freedom adventure. I was getting what I wanted: the desert sky, the rare plants, space away from the airline hotel. My lower back began to hurt, so I sat on the floor. The cement had been swept clean, tiny piles of pine needles in the corner. Then I dropped my head back to gaze at the sky.

'Reminds me of my dad,' he said, picking up a photograph. 'Though this place is like the open crypts they have in Argentina.'

'Your dad?'

'He passed away a long time ago. I miss him, that's all.'

And I opened my notebook and wrote, 'one hairbrush, pink. Steve's Dad, gone. Something has to get found now.' Then I pushed the child's hairbrush in the back of my jeans pocket, the bristles digging in, then separating.

When we got back to the room Steve cleaned his teeth and flopped onto his bed. I stripped down to my knickers, pushing them off with my feet, then dropped in alongside him. I lifted his arm so I could burrow underneath. His t-shirt smelt of washing powder and I wondered how the aroma remained so gripped in the material. He held me loosely at first, and then he must have been dreaming into something warm, because he momentarily squeezed me.

'Everything will be alright,' he murmured, kissing the top of my head. 'I don't want us to ever fall out.'

'Me neither. Ever. I'm just a bit stressed. Sorry.'

'Me too,' he said. 'Tomorrow will help.'

We were going to see a psychic. I closed my eyes and automatically hooked a leg over his, but the thick hairs gave me a shock, as I'd forgotten he was a man. There was something so distinctly non-threatening about him which I equated with non-maleness. I wondered if my sexuality, my lesbianism, was as much about fear and dislike of men, as it was about attraction towards women.

He made a faint whimper as he drifted. I didn't want him to go before me, but he had left. The room was muggy. The balcony light showed the shut vents of the air conditioning unit. I pulled myself from Steve, trying not to wake him, stumbling across the aisle to my bed. Finding the corner of the mattress, I traced my hand to find the entrance to the neatly turned sheet. Then I slid both feet down the bed, battling the tightness, using all my strength to get the sheet to give, determined not to let it flatten me.

As the morning light found me, Steve slept heavily on, mid-circadian rhythm no doubt, so I stood under the shower blasting water over my face. I opened my mouth to the spray, trying to get it to restore my hydration. By the time I came out of the bathroom, my face was tight, and Steve was sitting up, his eyes puffy. The pink hairbrush was on the floor, so I threw it in my bag. Then I sat out front watching the day take hold. The pool below was empty, the loungers all set straight.

When we checked out, we grabbed two filter coffees from reception, which after sipping, we promptly tipped in the bin. We headed towards METAPHYSICS' WORLD, the supply shop and psychic centre. It wasn't open until ten, so we studied the road for a diner. Starbucks was across the street with another only a block away. Even though I preferred independent coffee shops, Steve favoured the homogenous certainty of a Starbucks caramel skinny latte.

Outside, we took a table in the shade. There was a copy of *Arizona News* on the chair. I wondered whether it belonged to anyone, or whether it was a gift from the universe. Foreign newspapers still excited me. The headline detailed how the bone-dry winter had been another shot in the foot for Arizona. At ten o'clock, with stomachs bloated from the café's limitless free iced water, we crossed back to the psychic centre. In the window were advertisements for vortex hunts and night sky observatory trips. I felt frustration at not being here long enough to try one.

We pushed open the door to an intense fragrance and wind chimes. The shelves were heavy with packs of angel cards and dream catchers. We followed a sign saying *TAROT THIS WAY >* and found a partition wall with a poster of Psychic Madame Bonnie. Away in the corner, sat a middle-aged woman in a faded green velour armchair, her knees pressing through her black leggings.

'You found me,' she said, heaving herself up.

'Madame Bonnie?' Steve asked.

'Sure am. Come on in. You don't have allergies, do you?'

Dozing on top of a filing cabinet was a black cat on a cushion.

'Health and safety my foot,' Madame Bonnie muttered as she stroked the cat's whiskers.

'You go first,' Steve said. 'I'm going to see about having my aura cleansed.'

At the front of Madame Bonnie's leggings was a lump of bagged flesh. Under her cerise blouse, her breasts hung weightily. Her face was attractive, with high-pencilled eyebrows and soft lips and I could recognise the young woman from the poster in it still. She had exactly the kind of figure I would've once loved to draw at art college.

She motioned me towards a door. Inside was a round table covered by a greying lace tablecloth. In the centre was a hazy crystal ball and on the window ledge was an unlit candle in a pickle jar. I tried not to stare at the two pinned photographs on the side wall. One was of Madame Bonnie with a man in a tuxedo and the second, a blurred photo of her beaming with a young blonde woman.

'You've noticed my Hillary Clinton,' she said. 'Arkansas that was. The eighties. Before she got contact lenses. Never trust a woman who changes her hair so much.' My fingers found where my hair met my shoulder. It was longer now. Outgrown all its style, it carried no definition or clues.

Money didn't come up at first. Asking me for my hand, I offered up my right one and she kneaded it like dough. Her fingers were clammy. 'The goddess of the high has destined for us to meet.' As she peered at the lines running across my palm, she pressed into the sinew and bone.

'See here, how your hand bulges at the side? This means you too have the gift of sight.'

I stared, noticing how the pouch of fat did curve out.

'Your colours are turquoise, amethyst and rapeseed yellow.' Then she laid down a laminated menu. 'Take your time honey.' I chose the number three, a palm and tarot reading for ninety-five dollars.

'Ssh,' Madame Bonnie said, her chin lifting. 'You're all talking at once! Give me a break, spirit guides. How can I make anything out if you're all so vocal?'

She kept her eyes closed as she convened with the space above her head. The ceiling tiles were discoloured with brown water spots. I worried she was acting so I watched her closely, noticing her cheeks twitch now and then. Madame Bonnie finished meeting the spirits and dipped her face down, her white skunk-line hair roots facing me. When she finally lifted her face, mascara had smudged under each eye. Plucking a tissue from a box, she blew her nose, making a parp.

'Make two wishes then part the cards.'

My first wish was I would finish my story and my second that Dad's health would get better. Then I chastised myself for not wanting Dad to be better first, over my writing ambitions. Madame Bonnie dealt the cards then put the remaining pack to the side. Slowly, turning them over with a snapping noise, she breathed in and leant back in her chair.

'Your first wish will be granted.' She pointed to a picture of a vagabond holding a stick. 'I see success for you, you will make money, but you must watch out for a thin man. Balding hair. Bad breath, heart disease. Heartbreak guaranteed with that one.'

'Is the man my father?'

'No, I think a love interest.'

'But, I have a girlfriend,' I lied.

Madame Bonnie glanced up. 'There is a strong spirit guide around you. A female presence. But it's not a grown

woman. It's a girl. I hear her, she is passing on a message –
you have chosen to love women because of the lack of love
from your mom, when you were an infant. Your mom suf-
fered terribly when you were born. You were so big. The
current woman in your life – well it's these women that are
the problem. You know, you could carry on like this for ten
more years, in the same pattern. You travel, but you don't
go anywhere. There's men about, but you're blind to them.
Now this card here – you have change ahead. As a woman
you don't count on a man for income. Now, that is good.
You know how to use your tools. Keep a dime hidden in
your undergarments.'

She choked on her laugh, then patted her chest quiet.

'Right. Your throat is hot. Honey, I can tell even from
over here it's blocked. And your chakras, they're all over
the place. I can work with you on that, you see? You need
to get things off your chest. Do you have other ailments?
For another fifty dollars I can work on your body. Cleanse
those obstructions.'

Steve had spotted me one hundred and eighty dollars
already and I had spent fifty of it the night before. Now
ninety-five for the tarot and palm reading, but there was
the new credit card in my purse. Zero percent interest for
eighteen months.

'Yes, go on please.'

'Now stand up. Come over here, nearer to me, honey.
Don't be shy.' She dragged the table to one side so there was
a clear patch of rug. As I stood, I felt the twinge in my back.
It had been hurting a lot lately, especially when lifting bags
into the overhead lockers.

'Back pain?'

'Yes.'

'Then stand tall and tell me, who is your back up?' Madame Bonnie asked.

'I'm not sure what you mean.'

'Phrases in the English language do more than just come out our mouths to communicate. They refer or are generated in relation to our bodies. And so, honey, where there's pain, there's a supressed story. Take anger, well that's a knotted-up tale which needs unpicking. Your body holds the score – you heard that before? And finding words for it all can be our way out. You know the word intimacy?'

'Yes.'

'Well, if you break it down into syllables, you can really see what it means: in-to-me-see.'

I nodded, understanding.

'So then, *who* has your back?'

'No one really. Well, I suppose, my friend Steve?'

'Hmmmm. You see your spine is your central support. So, I want you to tell me who has removed your vital means of support? Who should have been there, and yet, was not? Back problems come from a lack of back up in your life. Or a robbing of it. Now tell me, who has got your back up?'

'No one.'

'Someone has. Is it your mother? Has she taken something from you? I sense she's somehow undone your core.'

'No, my mum's lovely. Though my father, he ...'

'Go on. Your father ...'

'He loves alcohol. Loved it, more than us. And now he is ill.'

'What would you say to him? If you could.'

I shook my head.

'Yes, you can darlin'. One true thing. Now, I want you

to imagine him, sharply in your mind. And, after three, I want you to curse at him.'

I stood there hushed. Ashamed. Blinking. Blank. A buzzing started in my ears, cancelling my brain. Compared to the lost Mexican children, those people trying for a better life by crossing the Arizonan desert, I had nothing to complain about.

'Don't take yourself out of the equation. Now picture him. Say the worst thing you can think.'

I pictured his armchair, his face studying the television.

'What was he like when you were little? Take your time.'

I remembered the day I had a bad period pain at my Saturday job in C&A. Working behind the till, I'd fainted. The manager arranged a mini cab for me to go home, and she'd rung ahead to let Dad know he'd need to meet me. Mum was out shopping and when I rang the door, he took an age to answer. When he finally came, I asked him for six pounds and slowly he took notes from his pocket, rifled through them. Then he slid them back out of sight, and I felt the driver's eyes hot on my back, but Dad seemed oblivious. He took out the change he kept in his pocket then arranged them in coin size, before slotting out fifty pence pieces. Then he took out the notes and found a fiver. Before handing it over, he wet his fingers, flicked the paper to check there wasn't a second stuck to it. When Mum came back that day, he asked her for the cab money back from the housekeeping.

'You . . .you little shit,' I said, closing my eyes, seeing the dark pupil, like pellets in Dad's eyes. My hands reached for my throat, and I began coughing, so Madame Bonnie shifted behind me, her palm pressed into my lower back as she began stroking upwards.

'Good, good, come on honey. And louder now. Don't hold back.'

'FUCK,' I shouted, fighting the embarrassment, the pressure to stay quiet. Then I felt something hot under my ribs. 'FUCK YOU AND THE FUCKING STUPID BOOZE.'

'That's it lady. Now, shake it all out. Keep on moving.'

Madame Bonnie moved round and, standing squarely in front of me, took both of my hands. She started to bounce on the balls of her feet. I could see water brimming round her eyes.

'Hop! Bunny hop, hop, hop. Skip along with me.' I laughed. I had been afraid of what she would do next, but now I had stopped wanting to feel safe. Madame Bonnie laughed and wheezed as we went up and down together. Adrenaline ran through us in a circuit, and I caught sight of her fingers grabbing mine, squeezing me into the present.

'That's it. Stay in the room,' she said. 'Do not let anything take you away. Focus on me.'

Madame Bonnie then hugged me, and I put my nose in her bloused shoulder. And when the room settled, she was puffing, and my eyes were wet.

'There, there,' she said, patting me. 'You felt it shift?'

I nodded, and she went to the corner and dug out an inhaler from a carpet bag.

'Now,' she said, shaking the blue container. 'Let's have a rest.' She sprayed two shots into her mouth then sunk into her chair. I sat back down at the table, trembling while she lit a candle.

'Now which hand do you use to write with?'

I gazed up, amazed she knew about my story-writing.

'I'm just beginning to explore it,' I said.

'I mean, are you right or left-handed?'

I held out my right palm, realising the mistake.

'I'll finish with the palm reading. See here, how your lifeline splinters, just there? That is where you left yourself behind. Now, listen to me, do not lose this little girl, who you are and who you once were. They can talk to one another. Help one another. There is a chance you will journey away more than once from yourself, only to arrive back each time. This girl, who was you, will tell you what is true, and what is deception and what is play-acting. But remember, she is only young, and she is used to being silenced by those around her. You must learn to listen, learn to be present enough to hear and encourage her. All children know the truth, they see things more clearly, but the girl hasn't developed the words for complexities. This is your job now. This is why you want to write.'

I hadn't mentioned to Madame Bonnie I was writing, I was sure of it. I stared at my hand and saw the line which ran from my first finger split into two in the centre of my palm, and then how it joined together as it neared my wrist.

'Does this line chart your whole life?' I said.

'Depends on when you start really living it.'

I waited for her to expand.

'So, I think our time is up,' Madame Bonnie said, looking tired. 'I can take cash or card payments. A hundred and forty-five dollars in all, plus I do accept tips.' She reached under the table and pulled out a reader. I found my bag and credit card, then placed it on the table. Although there was no beeping, the transaction seemed to go through.

Steve was outside waiting. I opened my eyes wide to let him know it had been a bit crazy, but wonderful. I wished him good luck, and he passed by the filing cabinet, now without cat, and knocked on the door.

In the heat of the day, I bent over and touched my toes. All the pain in my back was gone, plus my head was clear and lungs felt soft. Then I sat on the pavement and wrote down everything I could recall, how Madame Bonnie had released the past which was lodging in my body. Then I switched on my mobile. It was only eleven in the morning, seven at night in London. I waited for any texts to appear. However good I now felt, I half expected a message from Mum saying, *Call me when you can* – and then I would call, and Dad would be dead because I had sworn at him through the ether.

Sometime later, Steve came out of the reading holding two pink crystals, dancing them about in the air. 'Fuck, she was good,' he said. 'You know what she said?'

He stretched out his palm, running a finger over where it bulged at the side. 'She said, I had the gift. She also explained the reason I loved men was because my father had left me as a boy and there was a little me inside who knew the truth. She said, I could carry on travelling for years, while going nowhere. But change is going to happen. I should expect an episode of illness, and watch out for a tall thin man, but I would come out the other side healthier than before. I would live to ninety years old and get this, marry a woman in later life.'

Part of me had hoped Madame Bonnie wasn't a fraud, and part of me still believed in her.

'I'm sorry Steve. What a waste of money.'

'Yep, there was a lot of rubbish, but you know we did this little dance and she had me in tears before I knew what was happening. It brought up a lot, especially to do with Dad. The sorrow. This is funny though. You know what her parting words were? I have to choose whether to look after my face, or my body. She said men have to decide this before they hit middle age. I told her, I didn't know which one to choose, but probably would go for my legs if I had to, which made her laugh.'

'Why can't you keep both?' I asked.

'Oh, I didn't think of that. I should have said that. Here,' he said, handing me one of the crystals. 'I've come out really fancying a milkshake. Strawberry. I haven't fancied one since my mum and dad used to stop at the Happy Eater on the way to the coast.'

I placed the crystal in my bag and felt such tenderness. Taking his arm, we found the car. We would stop at a burger restaurant on the route back to Phoenix. Madame Bonnie clearly was both con-woman and healer, and it was complex how she could be both.

During the night flight home from Phoenix Sky Harbor International I sat thinking how once, on the radio, an author had said writing a novel had taken her the same length as a period of gestation. Nine months. The word 'gestation' came from the Latin word 'gestare' meaning 'to carry', or 'bear'. So I stood alone in the galley dunking a peppermint tea bag in hot water. Pressing my hand to my spine the way a pregnant woman would, I breathed out, letting my stomach press fully against my trouser belt. I wondered if this was also why there might have been pain, why my hips ached. Dare I believe I have a book in me? I couldn't foresee having a child, I just wanted something really good born out of me.

CHAPTER 10

What Was Over There, Was Now Over Here

London

One night, in an unfamiliar bedroom in East London, I became a bold new explorer. Her name was Terri, an administrator from Essex, with Russian ancestry and cool blue eyes. Out and proud for years, she worked for a theatre company and was an amateur photographer. She accumulated second-hand picture frames, which meant she knew where the edges of things were. Her face had the rare desirable mix of pretty and butch. Occasionally she would glance at me while a thought ran through her mind, her silent focus jolting a now-ness into the situation. When she stroked me, new gridlines lit up across my body.

For our first proper date, I'd booked tickets for the local playhouse. I knew when I reserved the seats the play was about a sex offender grooming a young girl. I saw it as a kind of test to see what she was like intellectually and emotionally. Clearly, I hadn't thought through how much the play's subject might impact on our mood after the curtain fell. As we left the theatre, Terri said, 'Well, that was a blast' and we walked on in an uncomfortable silence.

Miraculously, the bus came straight away. Although it felt good to leave the theatre's ill wind behind, the bus was packed. As always, we were aware of not being too lesbian in case someone started, so we stood in what I calculated was a friend's width apart. Then, without warning, the bus swerved, and the driver slammed on the brakes. I toppled forward and just as I was about to go down, Terri yanked my sleeve and held me fast. When I finally levelled myself, I blinked at her, then stared at the cuff on my coat where she'd grasped it. No one had ever reached out to save me before, and it seemed the deepest most thoughtful action ever.

Back at my flat, over large vodka and tonics, I felt like presenting her with the oversized lemon from the fruit bowl. I'd brought it home from San Diego and as I offered it up, her eyes rounded, then she said, 'slice it.' As we drank, the buoyant lemon bobbing among the ice, I got on the floor and removed her socks. Her very presence was sparking new ways of thinking. On her right foot was a brown strawberry-shaped birthmark. Lingering over it, I realised how flawlessness was a daft concept. Everyone had a stain, and it was better to note it from the off. Maybe this had been my issue so far? Thinking everything had to be perfect, or not at all. So I bent forward and kissed the mark.

After this, the days I flew overseas and far away from her, all I could think of was coming back to her arms. And when I was with her, the imminent departure cast a shadow over the time we had together. In turn, she pulled back if I became too intense, and I learnt to lean off so she would come forward. It was a precarious and terrifying dance. In the days and weeks which followed, I kept stepping on the plane, serving what felt like an entire world of strangers, still encouraging drinking as they flew, slipping into this existence with only thirty percent of me there. Then I would fly home to London, reconnect to the personal percentage I kept there, feeling kind of right when I saw Terri. I carried on trying to write, but couldn't concentrate when alone in my flat. Love was an emergency exit. I'd jumped out of it before, and I wanted to freefall again.

Falling in love was painful and things were often difficult between us. Terri sometimes felt offshore, or unsure about me as I nudged her towards becoming my dependable anchor. I couldn't know this was a lot to ask. She was the first person to tell me the things I actually said when drunk, how none of it made sense and it kept her awake at night worrying. At the end of a drinking session, all my nasty cruel ideas came out, like how I was convinced she didn't love me. That she was seeing someone else. In the mornings the accusations matched the badness I felt about myself. I should have figured out, how it was me accusing myself, me beating myself up with the poison, but alcohol blurred everything. It contained the dark, yet it lit up everything irresistibly. I was so exhausted by my behaviour, how it couldn't change. I didn't know how to escape the pattern; I didn't know how to realise it was a pattern, since I was so carved into it.

The next day I would tell Terri how much I loved her, say sorry, and try to prove how I wasn't evil. But come mid-afternoon the promise of a six o'clock wine would loom and the relief from knowing the monstrous voice who went on at me all day, saying 'not good enough' or 'nothing can change' would be placated. She or I would start planning dinner, and dinner meant the possibility of booze and freedom from shame. Even if I tried to hold still my thoughts, long enough to consider water instead of wine, my craving for white wine would've already wandered around the off-licence ahead of me, telling me to catch it up.

Also, I didn't know how to have sex sober, and now I'd given myself over, this time not just to drink and the airline, but also to Terri, I was floating in a Venn diagram where the three entities crossed and made new shades. And for the life of me, whichever altitude I reached on the plane, I couldn't see it, this routine of losing myself in wine glasses and people and places, when all I needed was to stop.

One night I got my wish when I found myself falling down the stairs of Terri's house. The *thud thump bang* noise was far from my body and I heard, in a voice like my own, a stream of suggestions: if you land hard enough to crack a bone, or sprain a ligament, you might hurt yourself properly. You could have six weeks off, grounded and guilt-free, you wouldn't have to fly to Shanghai on Friday in search of fish-less noodles, you could close the airline shoes in the cupboard and the passport in the airline handbag beside the sickening scrunchie. For once there would be no need of navy tights, or four a.m. alarms, or passengers taking an eternity to choose between chicken or beef as if their futures hung on it. You'd have to do without duty free vodka and cigarettes, but maybe, just maybe, you might get to be home, all in one place for Christmas.

My hip bumped the stair, and only then did I hear myself yell out. Stars pulsed my eyelids, recalling the freedom of the night sky and how the sun suddenly changed the corners of airline windows. Only yesterday I'd flown in from a nine-day SIN–SYD–SIN, working business class in a 'duty free' position, saying 'yes' until it'd become a hiss through my teeth. I no longer heard the passengers or spent time lip-reading or making up whether they looked like a red wine or orange juice type of person. During the cruise I'd read back through my notebook and found in handwriting I couldn't claim as my own, *I am a very bad stewardess.*

'Terri?' I shouted out – a reflex to be saved. This was not my home. It was elsewhere, and elsewhere was the last place I wanted to be. A poor part of East London where residents plonked doors over front gardens to stunt the weeds, we'd stayed up late, sinking duty free rum in mint-less mojitos. They'd powered me up, surging my engines.

By the way the wall was coming, it wouldn't be long now. Dust rose from the carpet. I thought, *when I come to tell this story to my airline manager I'll say how I tried my best, how I sought to break my fall and save myself.* I remembered my first flight, how I'd sat in the cockpit for landing and heard the crisp voice of the autopilot, the ground rising towards us: *TWO HUNDRED FEET. DECIDE!*

Decide.

I shoved out my arm, flipped up my hand and thrust myself forwards.

Brace! Brace! Get your head down! Keep your head down!

In rough weather the plane slammed the wheels on the tarmac to cut through the cross-winds.

So, I gave it my all. I encompassed the landing.

The wall bumped my shoulder first.

Then a thumping of legs.

Lights out.

Done.

The view the next morning from Terri's bed was sparse. Even though her flat was up a neglected street near Brick Lane, once inside it had a Japanese calm. As a hobby she took photographs of found objects in the street – an over-turned heel by a kerb, a gold party plate with a crust of nibbled bread – then had them processed on quality paper. She searched for old frames in charity shops, mending them with her tiny hammer, then cut mounts with a thin blade to fit inside. There were three hung on the wall opposite. Her father was an orchestra conductor, and she had grown up watching him guide musicians in European theatres through gesturing his baton, like a magic wand. This was as normal to her as it was for me to watch Dad wearily head off to the Insurance office.

I moved my hand and pain watered into my saliva glands. On my wrist was a slight bump but I could still flex it. The quality of light round the edge of the blind told me it wasn't early. I remembered the stairs, ending up on my side with one leg raised, my right hand folded into my chest. I had lifted my head, found no wet of blood in my hair. I remembered feeling confused how I could fall so hard and yet not damage myself. As I had fallen, time had stretched open, wide enough to allow me a choice to think and to determine what I wanted to do next. There was that news story about the boy who didn't die when he fell from the hotel balcony. Something took over his body to keep it floppy. The mother said he'd found his angel wings.

Terri turned over, then opened her eyes.

'Hello you.' She kissed me but then sank back, snuggling into the demi-world of waking. I rolled over and got up, imagining a bucket of tea to quench my thirst.

'Have you hurt yourself?' She studied me while I put on her gown, cradling my hand to my chest.

'No, I don't think so. I just took a dive last night. Missed a step.'

I wriggled it back and forth a centimetre. A dull ache now, nothing more. She shifted herself up onto her pillows, beckoning me over. Then she took my hand and held it tenderly to the light while she consulted with herself.

'It's swollen,' she said. 'See, here? I think we'd best get you down the Royal London Hospital.'

'Really?'

'To be on the safe side, yes.'

I didn't protest, it was a relief for someone else to make a decision about my well-being.

Later, when we walked into A&E, there were only four people in the waiting area. Within the hour I'd had an X-ray and we were shown to a cubicle to wait for the results. I perched on the paper cover resting on the bed, trying not to rip it, while Terri sat on the plastic chair. To pass time we played our guessing game of going through the alphabet, every letter a new city across Europe.

When the nurse swished back the curtain, she explained how I had a hairline fracture to the bone on my right wrist.

'Fuck,' I said in disbelief.

The nurse flinched, raising her finger at the wall: NO SWEARING. It was translated into many languages below, and I realised how much of the world congregated here in East London. Then she began to talk about care for the wrist and Terri nodded while staring at me incredulously.

The nurse's words sounded remote as I hid my mouth with my good, working hand. I felt upset at how I had sworn at the nurse, knowing how it was when the passengers cursed me. Then my guilt turned into this flooding sweet exhilaration. The fracture would give me the literal break from work I craved. Maybe two or three months. Basic pay, but still, no rushing off. I could own my days. Structure it at home in my flat, sleeping in line with Greenwich Mean Time, drafting stories and watching old films and new comedies. Sleep, I would sleep through the night and wake to my cutlery in the normal morning of London. Maybe Terri would come and stay part of the week, nurse me better with scoops of vanilla ice-cream.

Before I left the cubicle, I thanked the nurse and apologised for swearing. Terri straightened the paper cover on the bed and nodded over at me, 'you alright?' I nodded back at her with a sheepish grin, realising I was going to become very well indeed.

Freedom from the sky was a bit different. It was like the inverse of living. Over the coming weeks I refused to use the broken wrist, so all the strength withered out of it. I figured if I impeded my recovery, it would grant me more time off. It felt very important not to clutter up the space ahead with any obligations. I wanted a blank diary, a clear runway – I thought my autonomy would appear when untethered from employment.

At first I sat on the sofa, blanket over knees, watching *The Jerry Springer Show* with Hitchcock or Peter Greenaway films in the afternoon. Terri stayed over a few nights a week and cooked delicious things like spaghetti with sage fried in butter. She taught me what *al dente* meant. She helped me wash my hair, steady me as I got out of the bath, and I joked about us becoming old ladies together. Mum delivered ready meals from Marks and Spencer and did the odd bit of dusting. When Steve came, I held the pink cast close to my heart. He called it a *broken wing*. Terri christened it the *poorly paw*, and Mum, *the accident*.

One day Mum visited, and everything was normal until she asked me how it'd happened. I told her it was jet lag, but I knew by the way she asked she thought I'd been drinking. Of course, I omitted the truth in case she worried I was suicidal. Instead, I told her certainties which made her think I had a plan, like how I wouldn't be permitted to fly until I was strong enough to open an emergency door or prise a Champagne cork from the neck of a bottle. Then to change the subject, we talked about Dad's health and how it wasn't good. I described the intense itch underneath the cast, how I couldn't reach my fingers far enough inside to get it. She advised using the handle end of a wooden spoon. It worked like a dream. Before she left, she asked me if I was going to be all right, and I patted the remote control, believing this was what she wanted to see.

When the phone call came, I was in the bath with a glass of wine, my cast balanced on the ledge, fingers waxy and dry, listening to a radio show about psychic mediums. It took me a while to get out and when I got the towel round me, I heard Mum's voice in the lounge chatting to the answer machine as if I was on the line.

'So, Dad's gone off to the hospital,' Mum said. 'A fall. I'm going over if you want to come? I'd like that. We can get a cab. I'll wait ten minutes for you to come, and if I don't hear back, I'll go on my own.'

At the hospital Mum and I were directed to the Ladies' stroke unit as the men's was full. We located Dad in a bed by the window with a flapping blue curtain blind. He was all scrunched up uncomfortably down the bed. Shyly, I kissed him on his cheek, and he let me get close. His thin hair was oily, his cheeks soft and hot. I supposed it was the increase of oestrogen aging men produced, lending him a buttery softness around the jowls. It was then he told me to be careful, there was someone behind the curtain, listening to our every word.

When he saw my pink cast, his eyes focused, and he started trying to lift himself up. I could tell it agitated him. He had clearly forgotten about my accident. Mum arranged special diet biscuits on the tray table, and I sat in the grey chair to the side of him. After a while Mum went to talk to the woman opposite as she kept calling out, making moaning noises. Her name was Audrey, and I could tell Mum liked being over there being useful, smoothing her white hair for when her daughter came to visit.

As I sat in the chair, I realised it was too far back to be in Dad's line of vision. I remained there, kind of hidden, deciding to test his memory to see if he'd remember me.

'Where are you Karen?' he said, after a minute or two. And I delighted in this, in making him ask for me. My name sounded so distinct coming from his mouth. I didn't like it when other people used it – it'd never felt right, but here, him calling me back, I thought I could get used to it.

Just before Christmas, Dad went into hospital again.

The accidental holiday from the airline was supposed to be when I drafted some stories, but if only it had been my other hand I'd stretched out to break my fall, I might have been able to make a start. With just the left hand working, I tried writing. What came out was the scrawl of a pre-schooler who'd not yet learnt to do joined up writing.

So, I got a voice recorder and taped thoughts about the monsoons which made the orange earth run down the streets of Entebbe. I dictated memories of how I'd smuggled Viagra home in my bra from Delhi so I could find out if it affected my clitoris, but how I'd only got one hot ear. I told the wonderful story of the men giving each other a blow job in the economy toilet, how I'd opened the door with my pen, and witnessed this constricted moment of joy. I knew the difference between an enchilada and a burrito, cachaça and tequila – I'd heard the call to prayer across Islamic lands, been unimpressed by the Great Wall of China, yet floored by the Grand Canyon; I'd seen so much, but weren't these just anecdotes? Where was my story in all these swatches of time?

Mum and I began to form a daily routine of visiting Dad and the hospital visits started to feel like a structure all in itself. We would get the bus to Bromley then change onto a second for Orpington hospital. Dad was given a room of his own, and we would sit watching him breathe. Help him sip his plastic tumbler of juice. His lungs were filling up. Every day or so they drained the fluid via a tube attached to his side. The bag was hidden by the bed clothes, but when the nurse came I could see it was full of stewed-tea-coloured liquid.

Sometimes when he opened his eyes, I asked him if he wanted music. Once, I put my headphones in his ears, and he drifted off to 'I Want To Hold Your Hand' by The Beatles. It was their song, Mum and Dad's. Once in Spain on holiday, I had walked behind them on a cliff, and they had taken one another's hands. It was the only time I had ever seen them be tender with one another. It had given me the feeling I would never know who they were.

Although I knew things were serious with Dad, I enjoyed small liberties his situation in the hospital room offered. Like how thrilling it was to touch Dad's ears without him stiffening or pulling away and as he drifted in and out of sleep, I rearranged his bed sheet or read him sections from stories by Muriel Spark, slotting her sharp, odd eye into the infinite time of the hospital ward.

In the following days, although he didn't drink more than a sip of water, his lungs kept filling up as soon as they'd been drained. Two litres at a time, and I thought about how heavy two bottles of vodka were and imagined this weight on his chest. As I pressed my sternum as hard as I could, I realised there was no need for lifejackets when our bodies could quite easily drown themselves without the sea.

The doctor advised we should 'prepare ourselves'. He asked whether we would want to resuscitate Dad, prolong his suffering. We said, 'no'. I spoke with a Macmillan nurse and asked her to describe what was going on in his body. I thought if I could understand the science, it would help me know the timescale. She told me the signs to look out for, the way things start to fail, but how he wouldn't be in pain as he left.

One night when Mum went home to rest, I stayed with him and saw he was trying to move his mouth. He opened his eyes and his hand found mine, so I slotted my fingers in. He held my hand and after a while I got out my notebook and tried to get him to take the pen so he could write what he was trying to say. My sister arrived with her husband, my niece and nephew. My niece sat with me as I tried to eat an apple, her young warmth comforting. The nurse told me to call Mum. Dad's brothers, my aunt, my cousins, all flocked in. Everyone came.

On his last day he was so very porous. I wondered where he stopped, and where we all began. There was so much love in the room, seemingly from nowhere and yet everywhere as if all along there had been a portal which just needed to be found a window. Now I knew what people meant when they said love saturated the end of a life. His fatherly love was seeped out at last.

After his death, he visited me as a ring-necked parakeet. With an odd clear vision which came with bereavement, I had noticed how worn my flat had become. So as I repainted the walls of my bedroom, the bird had shrieked its green, yellow form from the trees, then clung on to the pebble dashing surrounding my window. He'd poked his head with that familiar beady glare, making me turn to find how the bird's red beak curved in the same way as his broken nose.

'Hello Dad,' I said. As the parakeet flew to a nearby treetop, something in me dropped, and somehow, I felt no longer afraid.

CHAPTER 11

Ghost Writer

LHR – NRT – LHR

The phone woke with Ray's Mini Cabs asking my whereabouts. Lurching out of bed, I turned to catch Terri's sleeping face, her soft eyelids mottled by night-morning. Without switching on the lamp, I went to the wardrobe, pulled up my skirt and breathed in to button it up. As I slotted a foot into each cool heel, I felt the floor pitch from only three hours rest. It was the same cruel motion sickness I felt from being woken on a 747 to the torturous lights-on in the crew rest area.

Before wheeling my case to the door, I went to the kitchen and switched on the overhead light. Noticing my perfume on the shelf, I sprayed a heavy mist over my hair, so it didn't smell of cigarettes. I'd kept up the cards from Dad's funeral. Especially the one which promised, 'This soon will pass.' Hanging my lanyard round my neck, I pressed it to make sure it was there. It was only now I took in the disarray: the cushions were on the floor, the CDs were splayed from their cases like silver pools and my best bra was on the back of the sofa. The empty wine bottles had been positioned by the bin. Only two stood there; Terri had stopped drinking halfway through the first.

Grabbing my work handbag, I leant over Terri and kissed her goodbye. She opened one eye and said, 'Oh, you're going. *Stay.*'

'Got to go.'

'Come back soon. Bring me something.'

'I will,' I said, struggling with the desire to crawl back under the covers.

Pausing at the front door, I rushed back for one last look in case the plane crashed. She'd pulled the covers over her head. A lovely low mountain range of duvet.

In the taxi, I encouraged the driver not to speak by giving one-word answers.

'Narita,' I said.

'Where's that?' he said.

'Japan.' The smell of the car air freshener coated my throat. I opened the window.

'Lagos,' he said. 'I'm from Lagos.'

'Humid,' I said.

'Yes. Very very hot. I prefer the rain,' he said, motioning to the grey November morning. He was a talker, and I knew he would chat all the way to Heathrow if I showed one ounce of enthusiasm. In the rear-view mirror, his eyes flicked back, no doubt thinking about airfares and all the people he missed in Nigeria. I shut my eyes and let my head drop back, worrying about how surplus airline fuel got dumped in the sea, all the food thrown away every flight, but then the fresh sushi I would try tomorrow.

My hair had grown longer, and I bunched it away from my ears to give me more room. I knew it should be up in a scrunchie and definitely secured by one before I reached the terminal. Many times I'd thought about what might happen if I refused to wear the scrunchie. At what point would someone actually say something, when would they feel it right to tell a grown woman to put her hair up properly? But the airline wasn't in the business of treating us like women, we would eternally be girls, ruled bodies on standby.

The cab driver switched on the radio. The presenter was asking people to ring in to discuss cycle paths. I zoned out, trying to keep away from the endless chat. How crowding it felt, all the voices and viewpoints, most of which sounded the same. So many people knew what they thought, and I had no idea who I was. At every turn my life did not belong to me, not in the way other people's lives appeared to belong to them.

Today was the day my life was going to change – it was a new mantra. Steve and I had been rostered a trip to Japan. He had been promoted to purser after a series of interviews. The trip request had come good at last, and we would earn over a thousand pounds in four days. I hadn't seen so much of him since Terri and I had become a couple. I knew he felt the absence, and I tried not to feel guilty about it. He was too soft to say anything and besides it was the common law of friendship: tightly bound when single, more flexible when either of you had someone. Still, the last time I'd seen him, he'd seemed detached, so I'd stayed up late to get us back on track.

The cab driver dropped me at the new terminal.

Constructed of glass, it was the size of fifty football fields. Even the lift to departures had windows so you could watch the journey through the levels as you rose. The self-service check-ins were bustling and there seemed to be an abundance of open desks. For once I made my way over the concourse without being stopped by a passenger. No one seemed to notice my untied hair. I stopped to buy a filled croissant from Carluccio's, making sure I got the discount, then shoved it in my handbag.

In the briefing room, Steve and I wrapped our arms round one another and stood for a moment swinging from side to side. My main aim today was not to let him know how frustrated I was feeling. All I had to do was go through the motions, do what was expected of me, and appear normal. There was talk of redundancy, but that could take years. He'd lost weight after having a bad stomach in Mumbai. He needed a haircut, I could see small hairs curling on his neck.

'Good time with Terri last night?' he asked.

'Yes, lovely thanks.' I studied his face. 'I don't smell do I?'

'Breathe on me.'

I exhaled a short breath up to his nose.

'Not bad,' he said, then took out a packet of Polos and with his thumb prised two into my hand. I put them to the side of my tongue to dissolve as it was against the rules to eat in uniform.

The on-board manager came in, closing the door behind her.

'Good morning everyone.'

It was Deborah Whitelegg, who had a reputation for picking on women. She surrounded herself with gay male crew and was aggressively tanned with a feathery fringe, blue mascara and coral-glossed lips. In her early sixties, she had fine, elegant wrists.

In a rare moment of stillness before boarding, Steve and I stood with the other economy crew in the galley. My heart palpitated from caffeine. Away from Steve's gaze, I went to the crew rest area, secured my wheelie bag in the cupboard, then took the vertical ladder to the bunks. In the stowage by the emergency torches, I checked which oxygen bottle was over three-quarters full, then unfastened it. Turning the knob, I managed a few breaths without reducing the needle on the dial. Oxygen counteracted the constricted blood vessels caused by alcohol. As I stole a few more breaths, I heard a click of a door, so I fastened the bottle back and climbed down the ladder.

Calmly, (so this was what it felt like) I walked along the cabin enjoying the empty seats with their headrest covers. A graveyard of spirits. My mobile was still on, so I took a picture for the future, when I no longer work here. The camera was still rubbish, but it would do. I could see Steve in the galley on the jump seat, holding open the latest *Hello!* magazine. I took a picture of him too, then sat beside him. He was examining a photo of a woman in sunglasses with her hand shielding her face.

'I feel so sorry for Jennifer Aniston,' he said, looking up.

I slumped down next to him. 'I don't know why you read that.'

'Kills time.'

Killing time, I thought. Only people who assumed they had masses of it would think to squander it, as if there was a surplus. I had done enough of this in hotel rooms, then I thought of Dad and how his time had come. I didn't know where he had gone, how he could so easily disappear. Grief wasn't anything like I thought it would be. I'd had dopamine rushes for weeks, colouring my vision. I had watched for magical signs from the natural world. Trapped in my lounge, a particularly frilly fly had bounced off corners in the air only visible to itself, turning at angles in an odd square dance. A tortoiseshell cat had followed me home and into the lift, spent the night in my flat on an old towel in a box in the hall. In the morning I'd carried her down in the lift and let her go and she hadn't once looked back.

Deborah arrived in the galley holding the long roll of the passenger information sheet. 'Here you are Steve. Everything under control? Who's working in D section today?'

'I am,' I said, getting up.

Deborah stared at my hair touching the shoulders of my jacket, and I waited for the comment to come. I was ready with my line about it being *too short to stay fully up without falling down*. I knew my makeup was good, I'd touched up the blusher only minutes ago. I was feeling rebellious now, no skippity heart beats. This is what it felt like not to be anxious. I stood back on my heels, bracing myself for the telling off.

Deborah looked over the passenger sheet. 'Karen. Could you please remember to use 40C's name, 'Mr Collins'. He's a gold card holder. Should be easy enough to remember as the rest have been upgraded to business class.'

I nodded. 'Mr Collins, as in *Collins* dictionary?'

'If that's how you want to remember it. Oh Steve, darling? If I could just have a word. When you've a sec?' She cocked her head, intonating they should speak in the cabin. Steve followed and I peeped round the bulkhead to watch. He did his serious company nod, while she explained something with her hand going forward. Of course, if Steve asked me to, I would put my hair up straight away. I didn't want him getting into trouble over something so ridiculous. I even knew where the hair band and scrunchie were in my handbag ready. But soon enough, Deborah and Steve were laughing about something, and then she sprang away, bobbing up the cabin towards her office under the upper deck stairs like a sprightly gazelle.

Steve beckoned me over, 'We're having a leaving party for Deborah later.'

'Oh, she's going?'

'Retiring, yes.'

'Is that what you were talking about?'

'I've offered to help later with supplies from the convenience store. Oh and love,' he said, turning, gesturing with his finger near his ear. 'I'd just put it up if I were you.'

'What up?'

'Your hair. Usually Deborah would have pulled you up right away, but she's asked me to deal with it. Probably because she's leaving. Sorry.'

I felt nothing, but then the anger came. Resentment replaced that. Steve had totally *become* the airline. So, in the corner of the galley I made a show of pulling out my handbag from the silver cannister. In the inside pocket, underneath my passport, were loops of black bands. I found my fold out compact mirror. Extending the elastic across my fingers, I bunched up my hair, then secured it. Then I found the scrunchie and tied it round the band feeling repulsed. In the mirror, my reflection was of another girl. I pulled out a few tendrils of hair which could be seen as wisps, but for me this was a small act of defiance.

When the passengers appeared, I guarded the emergency

door. My position was mid-cabin, with a view of the wing from the window by my seat. I stood alert with my back blocking the arm of the door in case someone tried to touch it. Releasing the slide mid-flight was impossible but deploying it on the ground caused thousands of pounds of damage, plus a change of aircraft.

I dreamt how on my very last flight, I would blow open the slide as a way of waving goodbye to the airline. *Hasta la vista,* I would shout, free at last, as I descended onto the tarmac flicking V-shaped fingers up at the plane. The unions had called crew out on strike against future proposals to create a streamlined fleet, with diminished pay and conditions for the longest serving staff. Redundancies. Under a thousand pounds for every year's service. If the management got their way, they would force staff from the old contracts and replace them with a cheaper set of crew. However badly paid the staff were, the passengers expected the same high standards. If I left, I would get eight thousand pounds. If I lived frugally, I could stay home for a year without the need to find work.

Wave after wave of passengers arrived. Most nodded hello, a couple faced forward giving me a cool side-eye. The minority saw me as invisible as the fittings and fixtures. Of course, I'd not met any of them before, however most seemed like typecasts acting out the same blowing up of neck cushions, or the endless confusion over where their seat was. I watched the eternal stippy-steps of them edging into seats, yanking the headrest in front so they jolted who was sat there. It was hard to think each passenger carried a beating heart and their own set of existential dreads.

'Excuse me. Miss?'

Male voice. Snippy. I'd heard this tone before, often in

business class. Resting my fingers on the emergency exit lever, I kept my body turned away. I counted to five, then seven, to see how long I could ignore him.

He whistled at me. 'Over here, miss!' he called.

I turned, slowly.

'My seat has been double-booked.'

He was a tall white man with a common face, prodding his long finger at a boarding pass. He wore the haughty manner of a tired business class passenger who wanted his trousers hung in the wardrobe at once. His large carry-on bag was by his feet and I hoped there would be no room in the overhead locker. His seat was 40C, and in his place was a cupid-faced Japanese man in a red sports jacket. It felt hateful, racist even, the way he dismissed him.

Manoeuvring my way behind the tall man, I lifted my elbow and did something I never imagined doing before. I jabbed it quickly into his back. Perfectly planted, it was soft enough to be seen as an accident. The airline uniform standards book read, 'No hostility should ever be shown. Under no circumstances should the passenger ever wonder if you are having a bad day.' The man stepped aside, and my lips pressed together, suppressing an apology. If I was going to take control of my life, I had to learn to stop saying yes and sorry.

'May I see your boarding pass, sir?' I said to the Japanese man. He patted several pockets before finding his wallet.

'I'm sorry sir, but your seat is in the row behind.' There was a distinct ripple as the Japanese man stood, grinning awkwardly, then stared up at the numbers by the overhead lockers.

'Sorry, so sorry,' he said, bowing.

'No harm done, sir,' I said, gesturing towards the correct seat.

Before 40C took his place, he made a meal of brushing the seat cushion with rapid flicking movements. He then sank into the warm seat, kicking out his long feet into the space in front. As he pushed his shoes off with either foot, I realised I would be sat facing him for take-off. And then too late, I realised, 40C was the gold-card holder, Mr Collins. He was the one Deborah had told me to treat like royalty.

The plane left the gate on time, but as often happened we were halted in the queue for the runway. This usually meant we would be delayed. As we sat on the ground waiting, I watched the series of planes turn for the runway. Each had a line of small windows along the side, every hole denoting a passenger. How many of us were sat here waiting, how many hundreds and thousands of us airborne at any one moment? Then I began to think about how everyone goes to sleep, everybody across the world, rich and poor, they close their eyes in the dark and leave the planet. Little creatures, snuffling. The everyday had become so bizarre.

The sun shone starkly on the grass verge. 40C had now taken off his socks and was enjoying moving his lengthy toes. He bent forward then shoved his shoes under his seat in front of his life jacket. They should go up for boarding as he was sat by an emergency exit. But I didn't say anything. He could die in a crash, I thought, and I wouldn't care.

His feet now dangerously close to my shoes, still he kept his legs outstretched. Edging mine forward, I watched how far I could go before he noticed. He was pretending to read his broadsheet newspaper by the way he shook it open, highlighting his own rich island of being. In my brain I ran through the assumptions he was making about me. Something about *trolly dolly* and how I wouldn't know real work if it hit me in the face.

I tried transmitting one of my psychic messages to see if he picked up, but he ignored it, licking his finger then turning the pages fast, as if he had read the world before. As the plane edged forward, I stared at the blades turning in the engine. I never had got a photo of me sat in the engine like other stewardesses. The grass was vertical, it wouldn't flatten until the engine blades rotated at full pelt.

We crept closer to the runway, and I remembered the softness of Terri's neck and how I'd nuzzled into it when I'd orgasmed on the front room floor last night. I pulled at the thread of this memory for as long as I could get it to stretch. It was one of our special parties for two which happened before every long trip. Each time we fooled ourselves into thinking the morning would never come as we swayed to music, the red lights flashing in the distance on top of the Canary Wharf high-rises.

Only a couple of seconds must have passed, but when I opened my eyes 40C was staring, and then he looked away. I brushed the corner of my mouth as if rubbing a faint itch, but I had dribbled a little. I examined the other passengers to see if they'd noticed my falling asleep, but most had their eyes shut.

Now on the runway, jolting over the bumps, the engines turned so fast the blades in the engine formed a solid blur. Keeping my eyes fixed on how the lines of the overhead lockers ran, I was sure to keep awake, but when I next opened my eyes we were already in the clouds. I waited for the turbulence, but we made it through to the sunlit blue without a bump.

Later, during the meal service, while passing 40C his dinner tray, I accidentally knocked the edge of his glass, spilling red wine over his leg. I truly hadn't meant to do it, but I had been nervous of him should he report me sleeping on take-off. He placed his tray on the carpet and then got right up, dabbing at his trousers with a tissue. I'd experienced this phenomenon before, how energy collected round specific passengers, like wasps around fallen apples under fruit trees. I insisted on getting the dry cleaning wipes from business class and when I returned, I apologised as sincerely as I could muster.

'So, what's going on with you? First the hair, now the accident . . .' Steve said.

'Nothing.' I stood very still, thinking remorse would come. Surely it would come for Steve. This was *my* Steve. I loved him. But no true sentiment arrived.

'I don't feel quite right,' I said. 'I think I might have to stay in later.'

'You're probably knackered,' he said, giving my arm a quick squeeze. 'Deborah's having the room party though. This is her last trip. You can't miss it. She says she's buying the first round at The Truck. And I don't want to be stuck on my own with the captain and first officer going on about the price of beer and their RAF wives' pensions. You're coming out tonight, whether you like it or not. It's purser's orders.'

Before landing Steve opened a drinks trolley and pulled out a miniature of vodka. He cracked the lid and doused the galley surface liberally. Then he ripped off blue roll and wiped the work top in vigorous circles until the counter tops shone.

The coach journey from the airport was quiet as crew plugged music in their ears and reclined their seats. Most of it was grey motorway with un-Japanese looking trees. It wasn't until we passed the Christmas-themed love hotel that Steve shouted 'SEX' for everyone's amusement.

We drove into the village of Narita, passing thin roads lined with slim green bicycle lanes and old telegraph poles with phone lines dangling across the streets. The bus took a left at McDonald's and parked opposite Keisei rail station for Hotel Mercure Narita. I wanted to visit the Narita-san-Shinshoji Temple as well as sample a real Japanese restaurant. If I did leave, this might be my last trip to Japan, as they were hardly ever rostered.

In the hotel foyer, the sight of the Japanese receptionist with his name badge – *Shiraha* – created a longing for the elation which these foreign details had once brought. He was nearly six foot, thin and wiry, and from his pale sunken eyes, he didn't see daylight much.

Steve said he was going to help Deborah set up the room party, and I was glad I'd get time to myself. Inside my room, I kicked off my shoes, then stared at the waffle material night-shirt folded into a square on the bed. Then I inspected the hotel notepad, the pencil balanced on top. I remembered from previous trips how the small pillows were full of quickly vanished air compared to American hotels. I got down on the carpet and opened the door to the mini bar and found space for milk from the plane.

From above came a drilling sound, and I got a bad feeling about the night ahead. Sensing a change in the light, as if a figure were crossing by the window, I turned round. The room was empty. I slid open the mirrored wardrobe to check inside. I felt the hotel room didn't like me, the coat hangers were those which wouldn't detach from the rail. A tapping noise started up, like a hammer nailing a tack. Or was it a typewriter next door? Was there an author in the next room? Should I ask to change rooms? What if the noise went on continuously? The airline vetted the hotels to make sure they were quiet enough for rest.

The noise subsided and so I sat on the bed. Only now could I think. I studied my work shoes. The front of the leather bulged where my toes pushed out, but I refused to buy a new pair because I wanted to leave. I opened my note-book and found what I'd last written: 'a passenger was found smuggling pigeons down his trousers into Melbourne. Write this into a story about trapped birds.' I was still in the same position as when I'd joined the airline. I wanted to fulfil my life as a creative, but where was my way in?

I showered and changed into my party outfit: bootleg jeans and a plain black top. It wasn't my style, but it was comfy, and I could get the zip up. I found my mobile. No text from Terri, which was unlike her. She always made sure there was one ready to ping into my phone for my arrival. I hoped she hadn't died. It would be just my misfortune to have a dead lover. Though, it would be something to write about. Powering up my laptop, I typed in her name, then added DIED? but the search engine was Japanese Google.

I threw my dirty work shirt in the suitcase. The heat from outside the window radiated in through the glass, warming the net curtains so they gave off a dusty smell. I sat back in the desk chair and cracked open a Diet Coke, then poured vodka into the glass, then got up and went into the earthquake-proof bathroom and poured it down the toilet.

Moving the net from the window I watched the road outside the 7-Eleven convenience store. Japanese salarymen rushed from the train station and two schoolgirls in pleated skirts, knee high socks and face masks walked arm in arm under a white umbrella. Then the tapping started again, and I needed to do something with my hands, so I found the miniature ironing board in the cupboard and erected it on the floor. One foot high. Kneeling on the carpet, my stomach rested on the tops of my legs. Then I pulled out my return shirt, sniffed it – washing powder, home – and ironed it, following the original lines in the sleeves to get the crisp shoulders. I hung it in the wardrobe, attached my name badge, then closed the door. Opening a stolen carton of Oolong tea from the plane, I wondered if this was the room of the stewardess who had killed herself. Surely, they wouldn't give us that room?

I wondered about her for too long and realised I was spooking myself, so did my makeup and retrieved my room key. The lift was all the way at the other end of the corridor. Due to risk of earthquakes, the hotel only had three storeys, and the building seemed friendlier because of it.

Pressing my ear to the door of room 303, I heard voices. A stewardess from first class answered as a burst of laughter sprang out behind her. The décor was the same as my bedroom – tepid green walls, muted lampshades, burnished metal handles on the drawers – but as I stepped in over the legs of the crew, it was triple the size because of the sofa area and kitchenette.

Most of the crew were on the beds, or cross-legged on the floor. The captain and first officer leant against the far wall holding cans of ale. They were often separate, as if the flight deck door remained bolted even when off the plane. Over by the window on the sofa, Deborah was pouring wine in a ruffled off-the-shoulder top which showed crepey skin between her throat and chest.

'There you are, darling,' Deborah said, patting the seat cushion. 'Come sit here. You know, I only found out from Steve just now, how you want to write stories. Who knew one of my crew was so talented. They do say everyone has a book in them, don't they? You know, my best pal Keith, the very last thing he said to me was, *Deborah, you should write it all down. Yours would be a bestseller.*'

'Oh, right,' I said, glancing at Steve who was determinedly not catching my eye while emptying Japanese snacks into bowls. On the coffee table was a tray of gleaming wine glasses. Deborah now seemed altogether a different person. She'd stopped wearing her authority and her hair was freshly blow dried, tickling her shoulders. Clearly, by the amount of wasabi nuts and bottles of Kirin lager, she'd been to the convenience store. The extravagance didn't stop there. Plunged into ice-filled buckets were bottles of white wine and rosé from room service, with four bottles of red on the table.

Deborah leant towards me, 'So, I hoped we might have a little chat. You know, you might give me some tips on how to get published. I'm going to have a plethora of time soon. What was I saying just then Steve?'

'About your retirement package?' he suggested.

'No, before that.'

'Menopause is no reason not to wear your hat on landing?'

'No, after that. Yes, that's it. I hoped, making no presumptions, of course, you might want to write about my life for me. Like a ghost person? Oh, what's that called?'

'Ghost writer,' I said.

'Yes, you could be my ghost,' Deborah said, picking up a green nut and placing it on the napkin beside her drink. 'I've years to get down. And so many photographs. Do you know, I've kept every roster since 1978. I'm sure we could come to some sort of arrangement, for your time.'

I watched Deborah lift white wine from the bucket. I picked up a glass.

'What do you think?'

I think I wouldn't like that, one bit, is what I thought.

'I've not got anything published yet, you know,' I said, as Deborah poured me a generous glass. I thought about how I hadn't even written one full story, just a few sentences of a first chapter. Over and over I had combed through them, picking out most of the words until it was so bare, I had to begin again. But this didn't seem to matter to Deborah, who was by now topping up her glass and getting ready for something.

Standing, she adjusted her top, then knocked a ring against her glass so it made a delicate tinging sound. She moved into the room, and I watched the back of Deborah's jeans and her small buttocks block my view of the room.

Coughing a theatrical hut-hum, she waited for the room to hush.

'Hello and welcome everyone,' she said. 'If I may have a moment of your time. I would like to say a few poignant words.'

The room fell quiet, and the crew shifted round to face her. I glanced at the captain to see if he intended to make a speech, but he simply brushed his finger under his nose. Steve was watching, and I caught his eye. He gave me his easy warm grin.

'My, don't you all look fine in your civvies. So, let's not forget why we are here,' Deborah said. No one moved. Steve passed me a measure of vodka with some ice to go with my wine. I placed both on the table.

'As you know, today is a special flight,' she said. 'And I would like to thank you all, my lovely crew, for your fine

234

service on the exceedingly long journey across. As you know, my time with the airline will be ending very soon, and I will have to hand back my wings, then I'll be cast to the ground along with the other mere mortals of East Sussex. But fear not, I have a lovely home and a horse – George – to ride. So if anyone would like to share any thoughts, or perhaps memories of when they've flown with me? I know a few of you . . .'

Steve shot me a wink while Deborah glanced about the room. There was a faint titter, where someone should step in. Deborah picked up on the awkwardness.

'Of course, maybe I should have put this out there earlier. I'll give you a moment to think, in the meantime, who would like some of this rather slightly better than mediocre wine? It won't drink itself.'

As the crew raised their glasses, a small light attracted me to the back of Deborah's head. It was a tiny patch of balding scalp shining through her crown.

'Shall I do that for you?' I said, standing to take the bottle from her.

'How very thoughtful,' Deborah said.

As I went around the room, topping up glasses, fetching beers from the table, I wondered whether I should hush the crew, as they were all talking too loudly. Waiting for her audience to resume composure, Deborah picked up a wasabi nut from her napkin and popped it in her mouth, expertly avoiding her lipstick. Finally, Steve stood and lifted his glass in the air.

'Everyone, ssh, ssh. I'm sure we'd like to thank Deborah for the generous drinks. So, I'd like to raise a toast. Here's to you and your retirement Deborah, and may you have many more adventures.'

The group cheered and Deborah smiled, sipping her wine.

'Thank you, Steve, that was lovely. So . . .' she said, turning to face me. 'When shall we meet?'

'Meet?' I said.

'Yes, breakfast? To start on my autobiography?'

'Hmmm,' I said, picturing the small breakfast room off the lobby with the salty, but tasty, runny scrambled eggs and baby sausages. I loved having a long breakfast there using all the condiments, having a salad at the wrong time, usually alone, reading through old copies of the *Guardian* I saved up to bring away with me. I imagined being trapped with her until the hotel staff laid out the cutlery for lunch. How I would take notes, writing as fast as I could, sinking deeper into her past, her notion of what it was to be a woman, to be a stewardess. I knew she would have the type of memory where she would remember anecdotes, but never dip beneath the surface to convey all the moments of feeling lost, unsure, the guilt of missing so much back at home, of not being yourself.

'What about I make a few notes one day when we're back home?' I said, thinking of a way out fast.

'Fantastic idea,' she said. 'I'll get your number. You know, I can picture it now – my book, up in lights. *From British Caledonian to Now: How Deborah Whitelegg Landed on Her Feet.*'

The following day I told Steve I was resting in my room, and he said he was okay with that as he was feeling rotten from the previous night's karaoke. He would watch a bootleg DVD on his new laptop. It was six o'clock in the evening local and I had finally forced myself out of bed.

I left the hotel through the car park with my head lowered, wearing sunglasses, feeling conspicuous, but not in a good way. During the day Steve had called me twice, checking whether I was feeling better and each time I told him something more descriptive about my supposed period pains. He was always sympathetic and as planned, typically remote about the subject.

As I picked up pace, I rotated my shoulders in a circular motion to loosen them. The crew were meeting in the bar, and I'd managed to avoid any contact since the party the night before. Deborah had organised a special table with sushi. I'd hidden in my room, eating fruit and crisps from the plane in case Deborah wanted to talk more about her past.

She'd already told me how she loved gardening. At one point she took out her mobile and flicked through her photo gallery then pressed play on an accidental video. The camera focused on white roses, then panned in, not with a zoom, but by Deborah stepping forward. Like a piece of unintentional arthouse cinema, the angle then dropped to fallen petals on the earth and the camera moved over a long lawn, until the frame jolted up a tall house before switching off to black. She'd seemed transfixed by this, in the same way crew were usually proud of photos of their children.

The street air smelt of rain, the sky white and overcast as it often was in Narita. I took the thin shopping street, passing The Fly Bar where the gap-toothed owner inexplicably played a loop of plane crashes on TV screens. Narita was famous for being the melting pot where crews from different airlines all stayed over. Happy Hour signs in English were propped outside, trying to entice crew in for the two-for-one beer and pizza deal.

The Buddhist temple was closed, but still I stopped to check for monks. Continuing on, past the small traditional houses with dark wooden beams and shuttered windows, I arrived at the Japanese restaurant. The few occasions I'd been here, I'd stopped outside and peered at the window display of plastic shrimp, ramen, or rice with fake fried eggs on top. Each time I'd lost confidence and walked back to the hotel, stopping for a safe French fries and cheeseburger from McDonald's.

A smell of fresh water hit my nose. Round the side of the restaurant was a slim alley and I found a black wooden bucket full of silver eels curled on top of one another. If this was to be my final trip to Japan, I would have to go inside. Registering doing things for the last time was part of leaving.

I opened the door and stepped onto a highly polished wooden floor. A pair of men's work shoes, a set of wooden flip-flops, and small rose satin slippers were lined up against the wall. I wondered if I should slip off my shoes, but I didn't want to. A red woven mat led to a second door, which revealed a low-lit bar and a lone man in a business suit smoking at the far end. In front of him was a long transparent glass counter and a Japanese chef in a sushi hat. No music played.

Soon a waiter appeared in a long apron. Greeting me with a bow, he asked a question.

'Sorry, I don't speak Japanese.' I said, bowing with my hands in a prayer position. Usually, I derided anyone who made no effort to speak the local language, but here I was without one word. The waiter appeared embarrassed, then showed me a series of stools at the bar. Along the counter was a bed of chipped ice with whole fishes lined up, some with gaping mouths and jellied eyes. As I resisted the offer, he gestured towards a paper-slatted screen which he carefully slid open. I nodded, preferring to be away from the fish and the lone man. Inside was a low wooden table which I manoeuvred under, sitting cross-legged on the mat.

Soon he returned with a printed cardboard menu covered in spidery Japanese script.

'Sake?' I said. He paused, running his eyes over my face. He dithered, then left, closing the screen as he went. After a while he returned with a small red enamelled box, positioning it carefully in front as if he was measuring the even space around it. Inside the box was a tall shot glass. Then he returned with a ceramic bottle and poured clear liquid into the glass. Just as it neared the lip, instead of halting, he continued to pour, letting it flow over the sides into the box.

Puzzled, I raised my hand so he stopped and wondered how long he would have continued pouring. Was this where the expression 'my cup runneth over' came from? Japanese? Of course. It meant generosity. It would be a custom of theirs, rather like the airline's *kill them with kindness*. I told myself, *see, Japan is not so alien after all*. And as I lifted the shot glass, realising from the weight it was crystal, I lowered my lips to it, sucking up the bitter liquid.

Sitting back, I remembered what Terri had said not so long ago. 'I sometimes think that for you, the prospect of having another drink is more exciting than having sex.' I replaced the glass in the box. Then waited. I was alone now, and no one could see me. Terri wouldn't know I was drinking. But me, wouldn't I know? Wasn't this the most important responsibility out of all of them? To myself? Not to see me warped through other's eyes. If I couldn't live with myself, how else could I expect anyone else to? Terri had been right about many things: I wasn't single when I met her; I'd been cross-eyed drunk. Double. I'd been in a relationship with alcohol, and it was the booze that called the shots.

The waiter brought me the Sake bottle and stood it on the table. I sized it up, deciding I would take it slowly, in order to witness what effect it had on me while it happened. Something about Dad dying had made me less fearful of addressing it. The bottle had gold Japanese lettering on the side. With the paper divider closed, I helped myself to more. It tasted like weak wine, and not altogether pleasant. But if this were the last time, I would toast Dad. Say goodbye properly. With warmth.

Whatever I hoped I'd ordered for my meal was not what arrived. A bowl of chopped raw fish garnished with the head of a yellow dandelion, a long pottery tray with two mini chipolata sausages, a plate with what looked like a giant sea-snail, and a cube of rice with dark fish on top.

I wondered how hard it would be to suddenly leave the restaurant. I checked my purse. My credit card was there. I checked my phone. Still no message from Terri. It was four a.m. in London. There would be no message now until she woke the next morning.

So, I was properly alone. I separated the chopsticks and slid the sea-snail under the napkin. Extracting the fish from the rice, I placed it in my mouth. It was chewy, softly smoked, sweet and salty all at once. When I'd finished it, I wanted more immediately. I poured another Sake and drank it down, enjoying the small, measured measures. I tapped my fingers for the waiter, then tipped the remains from the box into the glass and drank that. When the waiter brought more plates, a small omelette with a black seatbelt, I worked out the 'belt' must be a strip of seaweed. The final dish contained six pasty-shaped, part-fried buns, full of garlicy shredded vegetables with soy sauce and a sesame vinaigrette.

After he had taken away the plates, the waiter brought me a brandy-type drink. I sipped it, thinking how far I had travelled to be at this table. How a girl like me had come to be eating alone in a Japanese restaurant in a tiny village outside of Tokyo. I pulled out my pen and notebook.

I drank down the sake and allowed myself to drift. Then I let go, and I mean I really let go, and I dreamt back to my bedroom in my flat and imagined a woman a bit like me waking up with an unsuitable stranger a bit like Sharon. The ink carried me off across the page as I discovered I was writing from a place a little to the front of me. Then a sentence flew into my mind, *I woke up in a foreign armpit.* I felt the excitement from the idea, even though published writers said you should never start a story with a character waking up in bed. But it was a good sentence, and the word 'foreign' made it thrilling. For me, I felt the excitement solely for me, a turning in my gut. So I wrote more, and I forgot where I was and was more myself than I'd been for such a long time. I was only reminded I was a person in a body when the waiter hovered by the paper door, but soon he left so I could start living through the words again.

When the waiter returned with the bill, I calculated it was nearly eighty pounds. Grimacing I put it on the plastic. It had been worth it, just for the inspiration. So I folded up my notebook, bowed to the chef and waiter then left the restaurant. From the shop next door I bought a fold-up fan for Mum's hot flushes and a glazed-green bowl for Terri. I strode up the hill past The Fly Bar and slowed down to peep inside. It was now rammed with crew from across the globe and I felt brilliantly alive.

Back at the hotel, I dipped my head into the bar to find Deborah and a few crew sat at two tables which had been pushed together. It was a sedate affair, empty plates on the table and a few large bottles of Japanese beer. They were gently chatting. Once up in my room, I rang Steve's hotel room from my bedside phone. From his tone he sounded pleased to hear from me and I said I'd go round in my pyjamas, and he said he was already wearing his.

'We can snuggle up like old times,' he said.

'Please,' I said. 'I've written something, you know.'

'Well done love,' he said. 'I'm so bored with this film about bloody straight people falling in love at Christmas. We can watch something else. Something with a beach.' And it didn't matter if he didn't get the importance of what I'd accomplished, it was all mine anyway. Everything was possible.

The next morning, I woke at five a.m. local to find I could bend easily to shine my shoes with the complimentary hotel square sponge. Touching my toes, I felt clear-headed, sober and keen to get home to Terri. She'd sent a text detailing a night out with her father and what they'd eaten. She'd written it in great detail as a way of communicating how much she missed me being there. Her words were exact, and simply chosen. Pink prawns, sliced garlic. Lime juice. Rocket leaves. A low full moon.

Outside the hotel, mist hung in the air, and I walked to the temple then slipped in through the gates to catch a bell ringing. In the garden to the side of the temple I watched a Buddhist monk rake a circle in the pebbles. He didn't acknowledge me, and I wondered if this kind of life was open to women. No one would find me here, shaven-headed in a genderless robe, silently creating patterns in moss and stone. I wandered around the ornamental gardens until I had worked up a hunger for breakfast. As I left, I realised I didn't really want to be a monk, I wanted just to go home.

On the coach back to Narita airport I heard the crew laughing about the previous night at The Truck where a Virgin stewardess had fallen into a ditch by the road. I felt both relief and pride knowing it wasn't me and how it couldn't have been, because I could remember all of the night before with Steve, all the details of the film, the take-away noodles, what time we'd called it a night.

At the airport I took Steve's allowance for cigarettes, so I could stock-pile my menthols. As the passengers boarded, I smiled, bowing my head towards them, enjoying their polite nods. Japanese people brought their own flight slip-pers and tidied away their debris into small sandwich bags from home as they went. They were the best.

Fifteen minutes passed, still with no signs of starting preparation for take-off. It looked like all the passengers had boarded, but the door remained open at the front with the jetty attached. I assumed there must be a technical fault which would soon be announced by the captain, so I left my position and pretended to need something from the medical kit. From here I kept one eye on the jetty as I rummaged through the bandages and cough sweets. I watched the Japanese dispatcher speaking seriously into her walkie talkie.

When I returned to my door I pivoted to watch along the plane. The dispatcher was now ushering on a series of passengers, and I caught sight of a man turn left towards first class. Following behind were two children with their heads covered by long opaque scarves. More people boarded, seven or eight, so I stepped forward trying to get a better look. Steve appeared, rushing at me, grabbing my arm and leant in so close I was in the hood of his aftershave.

'You won't believe this. It's only Michael Jackson, AND his children. About ten others too. Apparently, he's been selling his handshake at a hotel in Tokyo. To his fans. Trying to raise cash for a new tour.'

'Don't,' I said.

'Yes,' he said, folding his mouth into his fingers. Then he hotfooted it up the aircraft towards the cabin where it was all happening. Of course, I told myself it meant nothing. This apparition of a superstar. This artist I used to dance to as a girl. He was just a man with children. I'd met famous people before, worked out the length of Cindy Crawford's feet as she slept, lost Kilroy-Silk's trousers in a wardrobe, sung a song with Lionel Richie and never felt that much. Not like other crew who went to pieces. The truth was, and I would never say this out loud, I saw myself in a delusional way as a potential famous artist in the making. No, I would not feel anything about Michael Jackson. Besides Deborah had instructed us no one was permitted beyond the first class curtains.

I went about the flight as usual and each time I remembered he was there, I gave myself a talking to, about how there was still time to reach my potential.

During the flight, I found out he'd had to pay for the whole first class cabin, plus the first two rows of business class for his entourage. The cost of his fame was so immense, I worked out he'd have to have shaken thousands of hands to cover the cost of the airline seats before making any money. Steve said he'd heard it was five hundred dollars a touch of his gloved hand with a photo. It struck me there was a point where celebrity became so costly, so enslaving, its purpose was just keep everyone's payroll going.

After the meal service Deborah wrote out the break times and posted them on the clip in the galley. I watched as a stream of crew passed through economy, clutching their pyjamas and water bottles. Steve left me in charge while he went on his break, and I picked at a dish of beef noodles and drank Oolong tea with ice.

Two dings. The orange call bell had illuminated.

I picked up the phone. 'Hello, doors two left?'

'It's Brigette, doors one left. Would you mind helping me collect a few items from the duty free trolleys? Michael Jackson is buying a load of stuff and I can't leave the galley to source it from the upper deck. If you come up, I'll give you the list.'

'Sure.'

So, I was going to get into first class. Before leaving I waited for the other economy crew member to return to the galley, then I went up through the dark of business class. It was a daylight flight, but all their blinds were down, unlike economy which was still semi-full of natural light.

At the front of the aircraft, I brushed the heavy grey curtain aside and eyed up the espresso machine, the box of designer chocolates and dishes of chilled curled butter. There was a hostess trolley with folded white napkins, a basket of grapes, apples, golden cape gooseberries with paper-like lantern husks. Silver salt shakers and pepper grinders were set in neat rows, making me want to touch them.

'Thanks for coming,' Brigette said, holding open the duty free catalogue.

'What's he like?' I said.

'Really nice,' she whispered, which reminded me to lower my voice. 'Just like a normal dad with his kids. Telling them what films they can and can't watch. I don't believe he, you know, would do any of the . . .' She put out her hand, shaking it in front of her skirt.

'Me neither,' I said, although I didn't see why not.

'So, he's marked everything he would like to buy with a cross – but how sweet, he's put family names next to the items. Look, there's Janet! We'll earn really great commission, but it's going to take an age.'

'Don't worry, I'll find it all,' I said.

I studied his writing. Black pen, nothing flash, rather dainty and feminine looking, like the handwriting of a teenager. I went about the plane, getting permission from the corresponding crew to go inside their duty free trolleys. We had to account for every stock transfer. If anything went missing, rumours were security would come and search your house. Over the years I'd heard of crew taking watches, cigarettes and perfume. One person got the sack for stealing the loose foreign change collected on the flight for UNICEF. Often, I thought of crew as magpies, petty thieves who couldn't help feathering their nests with bits and bobs from the glittering world around them.

Ticking off the items in the duty free catalogue as I went, I briefly considered whether I should engineer keeping hold of it. Build an archive. But we'd been told, anything Michael Jackson touched must be disposed of – every plate, fork, glass, eyeshade, napkin would be taken off in a special bag and incinerated in case anyone tried to sell it.

Wasn't I still too much of a good girl to do this? This was my problem surely, one which stopped me from getting anywhere. Taking the stairs to the upper deck, I retrieved makeup concealer pens, foundation, perfume, aftershave, the two teddies dressed as a captain and air hostess. When I returned to first class Brigette was plating up a lobster and sliced mango salad.

'Would you mind passing the things to him through the curtain? I've just had a meal order from his cousin in 3A.'

'Do you mean hand the stuff *through* the curtain?' I whispered, turning to look at the grey pleated material by the jump seat.

Brigette whispered, 'Yep, he'll be waiting. Just say 'Mr Jackson. I'm here.' He's in the seat near the back so he'll hear. He wants us to just poke them through so he can look at each item. You may have to bend, his hand seems to appear quite low down.'

I kneeled onto the soft lino. It was not lost on me that if someone came in now, it might appear as if I was praying. Unsure whether to poke one object at a time, I took out three Touche Éclat pens and bunched them together like sticks.

'Mr Jackson?' I whispered, not knowing whether he was there or not. As I found the slit in the curtain, I pushed through the slim boxes.

'Yes?' a faint voice whispered.

'These are the makeup pens.'

The tip of a finger and thumb in a white glove came through the curtain.

'Thank you,' said the voice.

I continued, getting a lack of oxygen feeling. Every time I pushed something through, it was gently lifted from my hand as if floating away. I carried on until all the items were gone. Then I stood, one foot fizzing from a dead leg. When a black credit card with no name on it shot through, I passed it to Brigette.

'Thanks so much, I can do the totting up,' she said. 'Would you like to take some salmon teriyaki? We've got loads left over.'

'I'm fine,' I said. 'But, could I have a coffee?'

'Sure, help yourself.'

I found a coffee pod and slotted it into the espresso machine. After all these years I still wasn't first class trained and probably never would be. Brigette opened the cart and pulled out a small white China cup, warming it for me with boiling water from the tap.

Carrying the coffee carefully through business class, then past the sleeping packed faces of economy, I returned to my jump seat. I knew it was going to be the longest day because I'd seen the night turn to dawn, then dip into a sunset, then break into rays of daylight again, all before the breakfast service. I checked that the curtains to the cabins were shut and edged down my blind to keep the daylight out. The darker we made it, the more peaceful the passengers. Alone I sat, drinking the creamy coffee, feeling it ignite my brain.

Time passed inconsequentially. I pulled up the blind a fraction to stop me from drifting off. Today I would experience twenty-four hours between the several dawns before nightfall. We'd already been in the air for five hours and the day wouldn't even think about ending until hours ahead in London. The world outside the plane was entirely white, stretched like a canvas. Land, not cloud. I couldn't be totally sure, but I sensed we were somewhere over Siberia.

I did the quick crossword slowly, two juice rounds, and laid out the Japanese pot noodles on the galley top hoping no one would request one. We didn't advertise them because dried fish when saturated with boiling water smelt rotten. Then I checked the toilets for terrorist notes, filled in a report about a broken TV screen and still, it was hours away from crew rest.

I decided to walk to business for a peppermint tea as it helped with bloating. When I arrived, the blind was raised on one side of the galley, the light bouncing off the silver cannisters which hurt my eyes. The crew member wasn't anywhere to be seen.

'Miss?' A big hulk of a man came in, his head nearly touching the ceiling. He introduced himself as Mr Jackson, one of Michael's cousins.

'Can I get you something to drink, or eat?' I said.

'I'm still stuffed from lunch.' He glanced at my name badge.

'Karen, Michael has asked me whether he can come and look out the window?'

'Of course.' The sound of my name made me squirm.

'He doesn't want to wake the kids by opening the blinds in first class, so I took a walk, found yours free.'

Before I could take a breath, or explain how this wasn't my galley, Michael Jackson was in front of me. His fringe hung over dark aviator sunglasses, the black lenses snug against his cheeks so there was no way to see his eyes. His hair was jet black, sleekly ironed, shooting out in a feather cut. A pair of reading spectacles were slotted over the neck of his white t-shirt. His nose was sculpted, unnaturally small, like a woodland creature. The skin on his face was heavily made up, perhaps with the newly purchased makeup and his hands were gloveless with pale dainty fingers. I felt him watching me.

'Can I, Karen?' he said, gesturing towards the window.

'Sure,' I said, just about hearing the words. His cousin leant forward and made sure the blind was fully lifted for him. The sun reflected off the miles of mountains, barely visible apart from a few grey wrinkled tops through the snow.

'Oh my,' Michael said, turning to me. 'Isn't it all so beautiful?'

His voice had the same high pitch as Mickey Mouse.

'You know,' he continued. 'From up here, it looks like the world has stopped. Everything's so still and quiet. It's as if there's nothing wrong with the planet. Do you feel it?'

'I feel it Michael,' said his cousin.

Studying his black suit, recognising how his trouser legs were never long enough, I felt there was almost nothing to him, a sparrow of a man his bones so slight.

'It's like nothingness,' I said, hoping he would know I felt things deeply. That I was capable of depth. That I was more than this uniform.

'And everythingness at the same time,' he said.

Still, I couldn't see his eyes.

'Might you have a map of the world?' he asked.

'A map?' I said. For a moment I didn't know what the word meant.

'Thank you. You're a star,' I heard him say, as he crouched back down at the window, watching the bleached vista underneath.

'A star,' I said. And before I left, I turned to take a picture of him with my mind. The atmosphere around him was quivering, like heat above an asphalt road in summer. My hands tingled, lack of oxygen. *Map*, I thought. So obvious. Where would I find a paper map? So, I left for the safety of the cabin, but it was not safe or usual as I stumbled on the carpet, hit my hip against the head of a sleeping passenger, waking them, not stopping to apologise.

I could feel the importance, my heart pounding. I pictured the plane from outside, looking down at the sheen on the skin of the aircraft, seeing her nose, her wings, but no map. Next I was in the galley, passing my colleague huddled in her uniform cardigan. She glanced up, giving me a tired questioning look, but I didn't want to talk or tell her, how I was searching for a map for the most famous man alive. Because she might join in and the moment, whatever this was going to be, might get lost. Again I faced the open mouths and lolloping heads of the passengers and I rushed and then stubbed my toe on a bit of metal under a seat, and it hurt, but it hurt in a good way. I was here. Perhaps I could live in my body with ease, joy even. In Japan, I had written a good sentence, one all of my own. So I said to myself, *you are going to find a map for Michael Jackson and you are going to find your own map too.*

I kept moving, circling to the back near the whoosh flush of the toilets, folding back doors, vacant, engaged, red then green. I rang the captain who said he only had a flight plan. Only a flight plan! I sped round back through the galley. This is my life, here and now, I thought. And it is easy to get into the wrong life and feel uncomfortable and yet not realise that's because the world around you is not anything like the world inside you, and that's not your fault. So I took the other aisle making a full loop of the plane and found a rare row of empty seats. I stopped to think. There was no map on board, only safety cards and sick bags. I should go and tell Michael there was no map of the world apart from my internal compass, but he would think this was insane, but then again maybe he wouldn't.

Then it came in a flash. Of course! The inflight magazine. I yanked one free from a seat pocket and flicked through the back pages. The globe was flattened and split into several easy to decipher pages. The northern hemisphere detailed London, my home, as its centre. Red lines sprung out, exploding like fireworks, connecting the airline destinations across the world.

On the way back to Michael – I was now calling him by his first name in my head – I gyrated my shoulders, felt a lift in my gut. I pressed open the page in the magazine ready for his praise and enthusiasm. Clean sunlight filled the space, bouncing off the door, heavenly. But where Michael Jackson and his cousin had just stood was now a mere empty space by the emergency exit. The oxygen bottles hung over the jump seat with the smoke hoods, the strap of the crew seatbelt dangling from one side limply.

Left on the counter was a crumpled napkin balanced over an empty shortbread wrapper. One of them had enjoyed a snack from the complimentary tuck box. It must've been Michael, his cousin had declined food earlier. I stared at it, thinking of all the people who would calculate how much they'd get for this at auction. But maybe he'd left it here for me. Picking up the tissue, I examined it for makeup. There was no mark, no clue. It was just paper from a tree when it came down to it. The creases were already working themselves out.

Unlocking the small metal flap of the trash compactor I dropped in the tissue, then fastened the door. I went to press the button to start the compacting but halted. It shouldn't be run while passengers were sleeping, it cranked and crunched the plastic so noisily.

But there was another reason for my hesitation. Putting my hand into the rubbish, avoiding the muck, I retrieved the napkin. Then I found an unused headset pack and tore off the plastic wrapping. Dropping the napkin into the clear bag, I smoothed out the air, folding the top to save the DNA. Then I placed it safely in my gilet pocket. One day, I concluded, like Michael Jackson and his strange Tokyo handshake, I too might be in need of making some weird money.

For landing I shot my hand in the air when Deborah asked for any volunteers to sit on the flight deck as a treat. The spare seat behind the captain was fitted with a fluffy grey seat cover and a four-strap harness with a centre release buckle, reminiscent of the air force. The captain gave me a headset so I could hear the communications with the air traffic control. As we banked, I leant into the side window and saw London below. Shadows from the buildings fell over the Thames. There was so much to see at first, but then I made out a miniscule London Eye by the slug-coloured water.

We joined the queue for landing; the sky was congested, so we flew back over the silver bars of Canary Wharf and the yellow stick legs of the old Millennium dome. And as we rolled again, the view became sky. Once more we became level and I found it, the Crystal Palace tower, small as a replica toy. Then I searched for my block of flats which, from up here, would be practically next to it, but it was all too small and difficult to navigate. In all the years of being in the air, I'd only spotted my building once.

We left the holding pattern, and the high-rises gave

way to a long park, then fields, horses and mansions with swimming pools set amongst acres of land. A golf course soon became terraced streets, motorways and finally, packed airport car parks.

Two hundred feet, decide, said the automated voice of the cockpit.

All clear, said the first officer.

All clear, said the captain, flicking the switches above him.

The lines of the runway appeared, then the nose of the plane centred as we descended. Coming into land was ever so soft, almost impossible to realise we had reached the ground apart from the brakes and the slowing down.

After the passengers had left, I checked the plane for any leftover novels in seat back pockets. There was relief to their tidy litter, their gone-ness. The invisible transactions between us, where we'd soaked up passengers' moods, had now disappeared for another day.

Once we'd given in our checks, there was no fanfare, no one to meet Deborah at the door and shake her hand then present her with a carriage clock, to watch the rest of her days tick by. I said farewell, then we all dashed through the crew lane, eager to restart our home lives. In baggage reclaim my suitcase was parked alongside the rest with the yellow CREW labels. I kissed Steve goodbye, then passed through the green lane of NOTHING TO DECLARE scanning the partition walls, the cameras, imagining the customs officer studying me for signs of deception. Today I didn't do the special performance, the one where I appeared vacant, concentrating on pushing my trolley in a straight line a little too hard, just to smuggle in a few hundred extra packets of cigarettes. I walked tall, chin up, staring straight ahead.

Just before leaving airside, I halted at the duty free shop and shook my head at the giant Toblerone and two-for-ones on litres of vodka. There was a pause before the automatic doors allowed me into the public part of ARRIVALS. I waited, aware I was still being observed.

Along the line of bodies leaning on the rail waiting for their loved ones, I searched for my name on a piece of card. If Terri had written one and turned up, it would've been the best thing. I could feel the public studying me and my uniform. By the time I'd passed the coffee shop I would have usually removed my Velcro neck scarf, differentiating between the work me and the real me, but today I didn't. It was just a uniform garment, a piece of material which I'd finally figured out held no more power than that, because I was here underneath it.

On the tube journey home, I pulled off the scrunchie, let my hair touch my neck and slept every small instant, waking up at Barons Court to change lines, then again just before Victoria, my semi-conscious brain knowing the route, so I didn't miss my stop.

Nearly home, I wheeled my case from the train station along the high street and noticed lettering had fallen off the sign for the Turkish supermarket. Instead of Penge Food Centre it just read Pen F d entre. The words 'pen' and 'entre' were so obviously meant for me, I laughed out loud.

Crossing the road, the familiar rosy-cheeked man stood outside Sainsbury's with *The Big Issue*. I gave him a pound, then reached into my bag.

'Want these?' I said, offering a handful of hotel shampoos and conditioners.

'Go on then.' He took them, feeding them into his rucksack. 'I know somewhere they'd love some if you get any more. Homeless shelter. Nuns run it, up near Victoria.'

I agreed to collect more, and like most times, I meant it in the moment even though I knew I wouldn't be in the job for much longer. Then I said he should keep the *Big Issue* magazine to sell to someone else, as I didn't have the energy to read it.

In the supermarket, I nodded hello at the checkout girl in front of the cigarettes. This would be where I would buy them one day soon. I went to the wine aisle and picked up a bottle of Champagne, wondering whether Terri and I would drink it tonight while I told her stories from Japan. Perhaps later it could be a different kind of drinking, slow and measured. Food could get involved. I hoped I would find some command of myself now. If I fully opened up to her, I would confess how unhappy I'd been, how ashamed, and how I wanted her alongside me in the future.

In the refrigerated cheese aisle I sniffed the Camembert until I found a good one with give at its centre. After every flight for years I'd honoured this habit, coming to aisle number five for fresh milk and cheddar to begin my days off, while recollating myself in the chilled buttery light.

As I meandered to the frozen section, I noticed a new display of speciality foods: sushi ginger, Caribbean cartons of juice, biltong from South Africa. When had the world's produce begun to be stocked in Penge? I studied the king prawns and put my hand in the freezer, choosing which solid curls Terri would like the most. Feeling a surge of hope for the future, I chose the expensive uncooked grey sort, then headed towards the checkout. For once, I decided on one with a person behind the till.

As I unloaded my shopping the young woman clocked me.

'Celebrating?' she said, her cheeks shimmering with sparkling bronzer. She stretched her back, sitting up.

'Coming home,' I said. 'Is always something to celebrate.'

'You must get cheap flights?' The young woman glanced at my name badge.

'I do,' I said. 'But I don't really want to go away anymore.'

'Really?' She looked at me as if I were insane. 'Oh, I'd love to go to Florida. Disneyworld. L.A. Anywhere really. Your job must be so cool,' she said, getting a drift to her eyes. As she dragged the bottle of fizz over the scanner, it beeped. I wanted to clap my hands, wake her up.

'You know, it's not what you think it is,' I said, trying out some honesty. There – some true words, they weren't so frightening.

She stared up, perplexed.

'I always thought flying was supposed to be glamourous. And all that danger . . .' she said, then dipped her head to find the barcode on the peanuts.

'No danger, not really,' I said. But something in her had suddenly folded, I felt it empathically. As thoughts ran through her mind, she remained silent. Then someone clanked down a NEXT CUSTOMER bar, and she glanced along the conveyor belt at it – her very own circular runway edging towards her.

'Well, you know, it's had its scary moments,' I relented. Everyone always wanted to know how I must've nearly died. At parties, it was always the first question.

As she scanned the last of my shopping, she bit her top lip.

'You know, could you get me a cheap flight, if I gave you the money?'

'I . . .well . . .'

'Oh, I shouldn't have asked.'

'I'll look into it,' I said, figuring I should leave her a mooring line to hold on to.

When I arrived home there was a letter on the mat in a white envelope with my name and address written in perfect black ink.

'We are pleased to offer you' stood out at the top, explaining that I was being granted a scholarship for a fiction writing retreat in Yorkshire. Stepping out of my tights and dancing them off my feet and into the air of the lounge, the letter asked me to let them know by next week if I wanted to accept it. The dates clashed with a rare nine-day trip to Singapore/Sydney, which was worth a lot of money. I would have to phone in sick, risk being hauled into the office to explain why I was off work again.

Decide.

It was in this moment that a lost story came back at me. How Mum had once been offered a scholarship to attend a private school away from the Elephant and Castle where she grew up on the Peabody Estate. She said she didn't take it because the girls were posh and wore straw hats. She hadn't tried because it would have meant leaving everyone and everything she knew. But if she had gone, she might have had a different life and I probably wouldn't be here. I realised I owed it to her, and to me, mostly me, to change my world and not live in a half-baked one. I had misfigured what being an adult was. It was nothing to do with pretending to be like someone else, it was about being complex, brave and true. Somehow the airline had chipped away at my boldness.

But for now, first up, I was going to wash the smell of the aircraft from my skin in the bath. I would chat with myself about how things might look tomorrow. Then I would rest my head on my pillow, to dream, to sleep for as long as it took.

And then, fully wake up.

Acknowledgements

Where to start? My thanks, first and foremost go to my sister Dawn, who sat with me one warm summer's afternoon while we worked out whether my memories of our father were true, or corrupted by time and imagination. 'It all happened,' was the outcome.

I'm so grateful to my close airline friends Scott and Lorraine for helping me fill in the details about the years at British Airways. When the past contains so many blanks, due to place lag or alcohol, writing a memoir becomes as much about research as it does about conjuring all the forgotten things. Thank you both for trusting me with some of the portraits of our lives.

My intense gratitude will always be to Goldsmiths University. When I most needed it I was granted the *Isaac Arthur Green* scholarship to study for an MA in Creative Life Writing. I found out the news on Valentine's day, which just about sums up how I feel about this university in New Cross. I am indebted to my tutors Blake Morrison and Maura Dooley, who had faith in my writing from the off. They took time to sit with me, dissect my thinking, and help me laugh once again. With their guidance, something vital got released, which had somehow got lost under layers of fear and shame.

It was at Goldsmiths that I met many wonderful writers who have contributed to this book, some without realising: George, Maruna, Sarah, Brigid, Ella, Aaron and Naomi. Also Nicola, Elizabeth, Ingrid plus all those who listened, questioned and encouraged me in Blake's life writing class. After that magical year came to a close, I was lucky enough to become part of an offshoot writing group. Once a week, during the worst of Covid, we met online and workshopped our stories. Debra Waters, Jennifer Howse, Shaoni Bhattacharya-Woodward and Shelley Hastings, I owe you the moon. And I can truly say, without you, this book would not have been born with all its limbs intact.

Taking over ten years and more than thirty drafts to complete, finishing Lifting Off is a testament to persistence and blind faith. I'd like to thank all the feedback from people I've encountered in the publishing industry along the way. To name a few, the agent Abi Fellows for instructing me to 'own it', Paige Henderson who off her own back wrote and sent me a reader's report, thanks also to my friend Kirsty Gordon who read the manuscript and cheered me on, then summarised the book with a crystal clear overview. Lastly, thank you Laura Susijn, who has welcomed me back so wholeheartedly to the Susijn Agency.

A massive thank you to my friend Evie Wyld for always being there and demonstrating her firm belief in my writing, plus letting me wang on over long dinners. Thank you, Jamie Coleman who has offered so much expert advice and practical knowledge, who could see what the book was trying to do when I'd lost sight, and gave me great ideas for the structure. I really can't thank you both enough.

Thank you to the Society of Authors for awarding me The Authors' Foundation Grant for a work in progress. It arrived just when I was running out of energy and lifted me over the finishing line.

My friends continue to carry and amuse me, and for that I am grateful. My thanks to the very best of friends Jane Dinmore, who encourages me to make art, and Karn Christensen, who encourages me to make Barbara Brownskirt films. Elaine and Charlotte for housing us in Andalucia and allowing me to sit naked in the fig laden writing studio (it was hot!) My life-long best pals from school who've witnessed my many incarnations, thank you Kate and Emma. Thanks to Gloria and Vivian for their generous use of their apartment in the South of France. Sebastian Walker for laughing about it all, and Adam Morris who allows me to go in deep.

The dynamic Paul Burston has been invaluable in helping this book find its home at Muswell Press. Your support Paul, not only to me, but the UK LGBTQ+ writing community as a whole is magnificent, so thank you. Matthew Bates, a big thanks goes to you – as an early editor you helped by directing me to queer essays, which in turn gave me words for all the silences. You took time to meet me online and interrogate my ideas, therefore enabling me to go far deeper than I knew how. My heartfelt thanks go to my publishers, the dynamic Kate and Sarah Beal at Muswell Press, for not only your belief in Lifting Off but for showing me nothing but care. As you said, it takes a village to birth a book. Thanks to Fiona for all your help with the publicity.

A massive thanks must go to the book family at The Bookseller Crow bookshop in Crystal Palace. Jon and Justine, you have been there through all the uncertainties and still let me play with the lights when the bookshop is closed. You have offered wise counsel, listened and consoled me when the chips were down and taught me everything I know about commas and American literature. As an Indie Bookshop I have learnt how necessary it is to fight for your values, while retaining your humanity. You have nurtured my creativity and helped me develop the now very successful creative writing classes. I thank all the students who have come through the doors (and online) your writing is always a thing of wonder. Many members of our Bookseller Crow book group have become friends, and I'd like to thank you all for the continued support.

Thank you to my funny niece Charlotte and brother-in-law Grant. My mother-in-law Chrissie. My aunt and uncle, June and Jake, who housed and fed me and drove me about when I was training with BA at 'Gatters'. And it's here I want to acknowledge my deep love for my mum, Lily – although you won't read this book, thank you for always providing the biscuits and the new laptop this book was written on. Your humour, warmth and endless conversations were our life jackets when we were all at sea. To Dad, you'll definitely never read this, but I now understand how I wanted more from you than you could give. Writing this book has allowed me to gain insight into you, and I want to let you know, the part of you I carry in me is safe.

Lastly, to the one who is constantly beside me, who cheers me on and never questions whether what I do is strange. Dear Minnie.